The Homeowner's Guide to Surviving Foreclosure

by Teisha Powell, JD

Acknowledgements

To my parents, Beverly and Denton, who always believed that education will open doors. To my sisters, Bethoyia Powell and Petergay DeSouza. To God for the strength he has given to me. To Jesus Christ, my personal savior. And to my clients in foreclosure who showed me every day what it is like to be a hero. I am talking about the single moms who stood up to JP Morgan and Bank of America and to the single fathers who wanted a brighter future for their children and to all who encouraged me to practice law. To this wonderful country, America. Thank you.

Dedication

To God, Beverly Powell, Denton Powell, Petergay DeSouza, Bethoyia Powell, Shanice Wilson, Bianca DeSouza, David DeSouza, Kathleen and to borrowers everywhere.

DISCLAIMER

The book has been created for limited informational purposes. Fictitious names of lenders, clients and people are created for illustration. Although this book, including legal forms, have been authored by a licensed attorney, it will not substitute legal advice. The skills of foreclosure may vary and the book will not be able to cover every foreclosure issue. This book will be used at your own risk and comfort level. By reading this book, you are not creating an attorney-client relationship with the attorney who wrote this book. It is highly recommended that you obtain legal counsel when faced with foreclosure.

Table of Contents

Introduction
Why Are Over Five Million Americans Facing Foreclosure Each Year?

Once upon a time, borrowers and creditors got along. Borrowers would go to the bank to obtain a mortgage to purchase a home. The bank would check the borrower's credit worthiness, because the bank did not want the borrower to default on a mortgage. Therefore, the bank would require that the borrower put down 20% of the purchase price of the home. The bank would request additional documentation, such as two years of tax returns (this would prove income), and two months of recent bank statements. If the bank found inconsistencies with the borrower's statement, the bank would decline to lend the money. Once the borrower got approved, the borrower would only obtain a fixed loan, which means the interest rate would never change for the life of the entire loan. Property taxes and insurance were part of the monthly mortgage payment, which means the borrower would budget her income accordingly.

Then one day, the game changed. Bank CEOs and Wall Street hated tiny profits on mortgages. With fixed loans, and really good qualifications, the borrower would not default on the loan. Banks also recognized that only a certain number of people could buy a home. Requiring 20% down excludes a lot of people. After all, to save 20% to purchase a home may take a decade or more. Also, a husband and wife would pool together to put down 20%, which means less buying power and a lower profit for greedy Wall Street. Banks also recognized that, with a fixed rate over the life of the loan, then the profit became a puff of smoke. It evaporated quickly. Banks and Wall Street came up with a brilliant decision that would benefit them by making them plenty of profit. Profit became a big selling point for Wall Street and the bank CEOs. With more profit, Wall Street and CEOs could fly on private jets and they could purchase Gucci and Chanel and eat at fancy restaurants and take exotic vacations for the rest of their lives. Their children and grand-children could go to private schools. They would live the

life of the rich and famous *at the expense of the borrower.*
So the clever Bank CEOs and Wall Street figured out, let us
help everyone to get a home. Not because we have good
heart. But because if everyone got a home, our stocks and
profit would head through the roof. And banks and Wall
Street would be rich for the rest of their lives and they would
be happy, happy, happy.

And so, they set out to get everyone a home. Everyone
became a target of the bank. At first, they had to get politicians on board, so the bank hired strong lobbyists who
convinced both republicans and democrats who would
convince American citizens that a home was the best investment and it was the desire of each president (Former
President Clinton and Former President W. Bush) to see that
programs came out to help citizens to own a home. And
they did. By the early 1980's, conventional loans only required 5% of the purchase price for a borrower to obtain a
loan. FHA came out, and it required as little as 2.5%. So what
a brilliant idea! Nineteen-year-olds became homeowners
because they advanced their credit cards to obtain 2.5%
to purchase a home. And, as if this was not enough, the
banks came up with another bright idea. They recognized
that requiring a little down payment, still excluded people
from the pool of homeowners. The bank could make millions, if not billions, more, if they could include every single
American citizen or alien or foreign national that had a
pulse and driver's license. Imagine how much profit that
would be for Wall Street and bankers!

So bankers and Wall Street came up with another idea:
Let us just give *everyone* a loan who wants a loan. But what
about income? What about down payment? What about
bad credit? I mean, does every one deserve to have a
home, even if she cannot afford it? Not a problem. Wall
Street decided they would just have the borrowers state
their income. But what if the borrower's tax return does not
reflect the income? Not a problem. Wall Street would just
create a program for which the borrower does not have
to even show her tax return. That way, the borrower can
get the home. So, the 19-year-old comes in and buys a

home, with no job, and the mortgage broker just states the 19-year-old is in sales, making $120,000.00 per year. If the borrower did not have the 20%, not a problem, the bank would finance 100% of the mortgage. If the property was not appraising because the value of the home was too low? No problem. The bank would finance over 120% of the appraised value. Because someday, the property value would get to that number. What if the borrower had bad credit? I mean, if someone has a credit score of under 450, is she creditworthy? Wall Street wanted to include everyone in the purchase of a home, and that means even people who could not afford a home, people with no credit, bad credit, recent bankruptcy, and whatever would normally exclude the person. What an enticing opportunity! And so it went, the entire American population, or well over 69% of the American population, owned a home by the early part of 2005. And then because the demand for homes was so crazy, there became a shortage, which was good for the homeowner and very bad for the buyer. The buyer had to overpay for an already inflated home. Bidding wars formed. People would camp out for preconstruction homes for days, hoping to get a piece of the inflated home. And buyers had to waive their right to inspect the home. Or they, too, had to inflate their income to outbid someone when buying a home. The values of homes kept going to the sky. If buyers could not secure a loan within three days from the date they signed the purchase contract, they would be out of luck. The house would be sold. So buyers kept leveraging themselves, so they could get a piece of the action. Home values went up and up and up and away they went. So now, with an inflated price, everyone began to refinance her home. A borrower became paper-rich in a matter of seconds. Real estate values exceed inflation. It exceeded common sense. It exceeded any other investment that existed on planet Earth. The average home in South Florida increased by 30% per month. Why work? Borrowers could live on their equity. The entire American population became filthy rich. Inflated property values made American borrowers rich. They borrowed against property to do things they would not even do normally. They took exotic vacations. They purchased exotic reptiles. They bought exotic cars. They stopped working so they could start businesses or they stopped working so they could just keep flipping homes. They also stopped working because there was no incentive to work, because their home value kept going through the roof. They borrowed to buy electronics. They borrowed to do plastic surgery. The old saying goes, if a dog has money, he will take it and buy cheese. So homeowners borrowed and bought things they did not even want and they could not even afford.

But why not? The money was there and the bank kept loaning them the money for cheap and with no criteria. And then, the same Wall Street who bet for the homeowner to own a home recognizes that the bad mortgage product would not sustain the level of appreciation, because it may have already peaked (which means they could not get any more buyers. They have maxed out). So, rather than talking the politicians into telling the people that the real estate market was inflated and to stop buying, Wall Street bet against the housing market crashing. And to ensure that it would do so, the bankers and Wall Street came up with another greedy idea. Why not sell a bad mortgage product to a homeowner, with a guarantee that the homeowner would default? By doing so, Wall Street would buy insurance and other products that protect against default. So, once a homeowner loses a home, then Wall Street cashes in on that home. And so came the birth of subprime, pooling and all other exotic mortgage products: pick a pay, negative amortization and interest only. All these products were designed for the sole purpose of getting a high default rate against a borrower. By late 2005, the housing market had crashed and by 2006, people began to be driven out of their homes. And the recession worsened, and by 2010, this book is dedicated to all the homeowners who are facing foreclosure. It was not all your fault.

What You Must Know if You Are Facing Foreclosure

If you are one of the unfortunate American people who has recently lost a job, obtained an exotic mortgage loan like a pick a pay, negative amortization, or interest only; or if you bought in the height of the real estate bubble; or you refinanced recently; or you are underwater with your mortgage (which means the value of your home is far less than what the mortgage amount is), then first of all *you are not alone*. Next, rather than stay depressed about it, arm yourself with knowledge by getting this book. This book will tell you what to do when you are facing foreclosure. You need to know what state you are in. You need to know whether your state is judicial versus non-judicial. You will need to know who your lender is and whether your loan is backed by a government entity or a private investor.

You will need to know the servicer of your loan. You will need to know whether you signed a loan that has a recourse. You will need to know whether your state has deficiency judgment. You will need to know how long it will take you from the day you made your last mortgage payment to the day you end up losing title your home. And the reason for all of this is just simple. *You need to form a game plan*. You may be asking, why on earth would I need a game plan?

Let's say that you want to take a trip. Your desire is to get from Ft. Lauderdale, Florida to Las Vegas, Nevada. You figure that you'll need to take a flight. Now, do you think you would take any flight? Or would you take a flight that goes from Ft Lauderdale to Las Vegas? It is pretty obvious that the only way to get there would be to take a flight that goes to Las Vegas. What is my point? If you are facing foreclosure, you need a game plan. You need some form of strategy. Your strategy may include saving your home, renegotiation with the lender, avoiding a deficiency judgment, or living rent free. By obtaining a strategy, you will save yourself a lot of headaches. Also, once you are prepared to handle your foreclosure crisis, you will feel a lot better. Trust me. I've seen many homeowners in this foreclosure crisis and the ones that are prepared are doing much better than the ones that are just in dump fold.

How Will this Book Help You?

This book will help you if you are in a judicial or non-judicial foreclosure state, as it covers information on both types of foreclosures. This book will help you by arming you with information. Knowledge is power and since foreclosure is perhaps something you have never experienced before, you will need to obtain the knowledge that will help you to have a better understanding of foreclosure. This book will help you if you decide that you want to renegotiate your loan terms with your lenders. It will help you decide whether you can defend foreclosure on your own or whether you should hire counsel. It will help you to see alternatives to foreclosure, like a deed in lieu, a short sale, and a short pay-refinance. It will also help you to delay your foreclosure if you decide that living rent free will help you save money. It will also help you understand the different types of bankruptcy and how they can help you save your home. If you are not yet in foreclosure and still have good credit, but you recognize that you will be facing foreclosure in the near future, this book will provide information that can help you to save your home by obtaining a new loan and cheaper payments. If you want to walk away from your home with no judgment, and no IRS taxes owed, this book will explain to you how you can negotiate to walk away from your foreclosure. This book will also provide you with additional information beyond the book that can help your foreclosure situation. If you have no cash, and no equity, but want to save your home, this book will help you. This book will help you if you want to learn more about the loan modification and how to obtain one. This book will cover many areas in foreclosure. It will show you how to bank bucks while in foreclosure. Read on.

Which Homeowner and Investors Will Be Facing Foreclosure?

My firm has been handling foreclosure for years. I have researched and spoken with many experts in this field.

Because I am an attorney and former real estate investor, I tend to see things analytically. I like to show people probability because, well that is just one way you can narrow things down or find victims of foreclosure. However, please take it with a grain of salt. The thing about foreclosure is that you may be okay today, but after a year or so paying on your mortgage, you will find yourself in foreclosure. That is just how foreclosure works. No one buys a house with the anticipation of going into foreclosure. Unless of course, you are the banker betting against the borrower. But that will be another story for another book. Foreclosure may have to do more with the timing of when you purchase the property or the product you obtained or outside circumstances, like the recession, globalization, technology, and supply and demand. So, I just want to show you this probability so you can have an idea whether this foreclosure tsunami will affect you. And, if not, it may affect the neighborhood you live in or someone you know. I noticed a few things with the foreclosure trend. It had to do with the type of loan the person obtained and the year the person purchased or refinanced and the location and the type of lender. Here is the probability of where a person falls with regard to going into foreclosure:

1. You purchased or refinanced your home during the real estate peak market. Anywhere from 2005-2009.
2. You are underwater with your mortgage (your home is worth less than your mortgage).
3. You recently lost a job, or your took a big pay cut, which means you may not be able to keep up with your mortgage payment.
4. You obtained an interest-only loan that is scheduled to adjust and, with the new payments, you will not be able to pay for the loan.
5. You bought a loan based upon a stated income loan or a stated income and stated asset. (If you exaggerated your income to obtain the loan, then you are perhaps in a home that you cannot afford).
6. The bank or the mortgage broker told you to close on the loan and they promised to refinance you out of it

soon. Well, you know today the bankers lied. The same bank that promised to refinance you will be suing you for the note. It cannot make good on its promise because the value of the homes is no longer there. What the bank should have said is that it would refinance you only if the property is worth more. But I guess the bank was betting that the property would go to the sky. Greed trumps common sense.

7. You bought the home on speculation and you had every intention of flipping it.

8. You owned more than one property. In fact, you speculated on the real estate at the peak of the real estate market. Most people think that real estate will just keep going to the sky. They really do not understand that real estate is peak *and* valley. It goes up and it goes down. I mean how our future generation would get to afford a home, if it kept going to the sky? Don't you think that supply and demand will trump your greed?

9. You failed to escrow taxes into the loan.

10. You are feeling the pinch of the recession and it is beginning to affect your finances.

11. You bought a home at 120% LTV or 100% LTV, meaning the lender financed all of it.

12. You bought a home with no money down.

13. You obtained cash at closing from the lender. (Most lenders allowed the borrower to cash out, because the lender knew that the borrower could not afford the mortgage. Of course, the lender did not tell the borrower that the borrower was obtaining cash because she could not afford the mortgage. So the lender gave the borrower cash, so that the borrower would use the cash to pay for the mortgage. The lenders are not that stupid. How silly it would look if they put all these people in homes and the people end up foreclosing one month after the purchase. So why not give the borrower enough cash to pay for the next 24 to 36 months. Besides property values were going to the sky. So no one would be harmed by this trick and no one would sense that the lender released a bad product into the

marketplace. Additionally, the lender wanted to sell the loan, too. So no investor would purchase a loan that is subject to default or a loan a borrower already defaulted on. That would be seen as a non-performing asset. Therefore, if the lender sells the loan within 24 months, then it would be off its book and the investor would think that, wow, I have an asset. The borrower is paying. Unbeknownst to the investor, the borrower is paying because the lender gave the borrower money). There is a very wise saying. *If it is too good to be true, it is.* Ask yourself, why would a lender give you cash to buy a home? Is it from your good looks or your charm? What benefit is that to the lender? I guess we are beginning to see.

14. Over the past 3 years, you used your equity as an ATM and you could not stop refinancing.
15. You have more than one mortgage attached to the property.
16. You have a loan from a hard-money lender, with the anticipation that you would flip the property.
17. You purchased preconstruction homes on speculation.
18. You have a subprime loan, which means the lender bet that you would default. These loans include negative amortization, pick a pay, and interest only. Since the day you got the loan, and the lender had placed you on a high probability of defaulting, you will default. The loan was set up that way and there is nothing you can do to avoid it. It has nothing to do with whether you are a good person. Or whether you pay your bills on time. The odds are against you. The product is bad.
19. You obtained a loan with a heavy prepayment penalty.
20. You obtained a negative amortization from Washington Mutual, Countrywide, Indymac, Bank United, Lehman Brothers or pick a pay from one of those banks. [1]
21. You property is located in Nevada, Florida or California.[2]

---

1 I am by no means bashing Washington Mutual or Countrywide. But those bank folded because they had too many negative amortization loans. So if the bank folds, it is because it would not be able to collect on those loans. Unfortunately, any homeowner who receives this negative amortization product will, too, go under.

2 These three states have the highest foreclosure rate.

22. You feel you are at the verge of bankruptcy.
23. You cannot stomach making another mortgage payment.
24. You decide that a strategy default is your best option because you are so underwater with your property.
25. You think morally you no longer should pay for a home on which the mortgage is worth more than the value of the home.
26. You no longer think foreclosure is a stigma and friends and family are bragging to you how much they are saving from living rent free.
27. You think that life is not fair. Why should you pay for a home, when the borrowers who are not paying for their homes are getting a free ride? And as such, you made a decision to also get a free ride. You are just tired of doing what is right. And you are missing out on the strategy default.
28. You already spoke with an accountant and lawyer who told you to walk away from your home, because you will never make back the loss. And you no longer care about the hit a foreclosure will have on your credit.
29. You heard of people obtaining a principle reduction through foreclosure and you want one also.
30. You have officially dipped into your retirement, savings, maxed out credit cards and borrowing from friends and family to pay for your mortgage.
31. If you continue to pay on the mortgage, it will wipe you out financially, meaning you will not have any money left to buy food, to save for retirement or the mortgage will bring you to your knees.
32. You are working 2-3 jobs so you can pay for the mortgage.
33. You are more than 30 days past due on your mortgage.
34. You bought more home than you can afford.
35. You recently suffered some form of financial hardship, illness, death, loss of job or divorce.
36. Your mortgage payment, which includes principle, interest, taxes and insurance exceeds 31% of your gross

income. If you are married, then 31% of your combined income.

37. You obtained a predatory loan. [3]
38. You are black or of Hispanic descent.[4]
39. You obtain the mortgage with very little resistance from the bank. There has got to be a problem when you walk into a bank and you obtain a loan within three days. You provided very little paperwork and the bank just signed off on it anyway.
40. You or the lender exaggerated the appraisal on the property.
41. Fraud was committed during your mortgage, either by you, the lender, or the mortgage broker. Examples of fraud: a fudged appraisal. Your income tax was changed to reflect a bigger number. Your pay stubs were forged. Funds were wired into your bank account to reflect an exaggerate bank statement. I know in south Florida, especially in the Miami area, when the real estate market took off, many mortgage brokers thought it was their duty to commit fraud. They did so to help the homeowner obtain a mortgage. However, that was a disservice to the homeowner, because all the mortgage broker did was help the homeowner obtain a home that the homeowner cannot afford. And I am sure today the homeowner is not thanking the mortgage broker for the stupid home that is now subject to foreclosure. And yes, unfortunately, some of the banks were in on it as well. But, I guess, everyone was looking to see that the properties were going higher. And nothing would go lower.
42. You refinance your home just so you can still keep up with your mortgage payment.
43. You took out a second loan so you can pay the mortgage.

---

3 Predatory lending means that the bank funded a loan to a borrower that is unfair and harsh. This includes excessive fees, very high interest rate, or very stiff prepayment penalty. If a borrower keeps paying on a predatory loan, the borrower will more likely go broke.

4 It just appears that over the years, Blacks and Hispanic are profiled by lenders for bad mortgage product.

Creating a Game Plan for Your Foreclosure

Now let us say you are reading this book and you stumble across the area that talks about your probability. And you know that probability is you. Now what? Do you panic? Do you run away from your problem? Do you scream and cry because your world is coming to an end? Or do you create a game plan, because the next few months or years, you will have an experience? You do the last one. You create a game plan. Foreclosure is just an experience, whether it is good or bad. That is up to you, and how you want to label it. I have clients who have been in foreclosure for the last two years, and they do not even care. They are living rent free and they are not wishing that things end. They love the idea of riding through the foreclosure crisis. And they are saving money. For each month that they are not paying a mortgage, that is money into their pocket. On the other hand, I have other clients in foreclosure and they cry every day. They call me every day and every night to ask when it will be over. They cannot work. They cannot do any-thing. They see foreclosure as a really bad plague and that they will somehow die from it. They have this preconceived idea that everyone should own a home and since they are in foreclosure, they must have done something bad. They feel like an outcast. They think that people will treat them differently because they are in foreclosure. What they don't understand is that well over 7 million Americans are in foreclosure. And people think more of themselves than they do of you. This is a national catastrophe and to make it personal like you are the only one involved in it, is just plain wrong and stupid. Besides with that kind of attitude, you will not be able to make a good decision. And yes, you can purchase a home as soon as four years after foreclosure. And property values are so cheap. So be glad you are in foreclosure. You are losing a home with no equity in it. And now you can get one at a rock-bottom price. This life is not perfect. And things are going to happen to you all the time. You just have to think positively. There are many posi-tive aspects to foreclosure. I see more positive aspects that negative aspects. That is what I can tell you.

So you need to come up with a game plan. Your game plan should be done prior to the foreclosure happening. You know most people know they are going to be in foreclosure. They can sense it. The writing will be all over the wall. And if it is not, then keep reading the book and you will come out of denial. So once you suspect that you will be in foreclosure, the next thing to do is to avoid panicking. You will need to save your energy, because it will be a fight. If you panic, then you cannot think clearly. I know that foreclosure is an emotional experience because you are about to lose your home. You love it. You are attached to it. But if you really want to save your home, then live in the present moment. Avoid the panic and stay focused.

Use the following checklist to get started:

Are you still current on your payments?	
What is your property worth?	
What is the mortgage amount owed?	
Do you want to keep the home?	
If you decide that you want to keep the home, then once you answer the first four questions, look in the chapters that have to do with refinance and short pay off refinance.	
What stage of the foreclosure are you in?	
Do you want to keep the home?	
If you missed payments, then look into the chapter of loan modification (but that is if you decide to keep the home).	
Will your lender initiate foreclosure?	
If that is correct, look into whether you are in a judicial or non-judicial state.	
Once the foreclosure is happening, how much time do you have?	
What do you want to do? Do you want to keep the home? Can you afford to keep the home? Do you have a stable job? Do you love the home? Is it even possible to keep the home?	
If you decide that you want to walk away, then look at the chapters that has to do with deed in lieu, short sale, foreclosure defense (if is judicial state), deficiency judgment, Bankruptcy.	

If you decide that you want to fight foreclosure so you can buy time or you want to still save your home, then look into foreclosure defense, bankruptcy, reinstatement, forbearance, loan modification, and short pay-refinance FHA.	
Find out what state you reside in because you will need to know which type of foreclosure will take place against your home.	
Find out what you want? You have got to come up with a plan that is tailored your needs. Only you know what type of stress you can handle. And only you know how much anxiety you can handle. No one else will know that for you. And only you know what is the best decision for you and your family. And no expert will have that information for you.	
Is saving the home feasible or is walking away feasible?	
Weigh the pros and cons on keeping the home versus walking away.	
Perhaps foreclosure is not ideal. I mean, everyone purchases the home with the desire to live there permanently. But now that you are in foreclosure, figure out what you want from it.	
Do you want to live there rent free and save some money	
Once you come up with a game plan, make sure that you are flexible because things will not always work in your favor. Let us say you want to do a deed in lieu, but your lender says no. do you just give up then? Or do you play it by ear and come up with another plan? I would say your best bet is to have at least three plans. That way, if one does not go as planned, you can go to the next one.	

Can You Keep Your Home or Must You Walk Away?

Let us say you are in foreclosure, there are only two options for you. You either keep the home (by saving it) or you lose the home, which means you walk away or the lender forecloses. There is no in between. You will either get out of foreclosure or you will give in to foreclosure. What you may have a little control over is which one you would rather do. You might see the foreclosure as a blessing because you could not pay the mortgage anyway. In that case you walk away. You might see foreclosure as a curse and you will do what you can to save your home. In that case, you keep it.

Whatever your reasons are for keeping the home, once you make that decision, you need to now come up with a game plan. You can keep the home through a loan modification, a forbearance, a short pay off refinance, negotiation new loan terms, redemption, reinstatement, refinance, or bankruptcy.

If you decide to walk away then you should look at some of the positives. You can choose to delay the foreclosure. Why? To buy time. Why on earth would someone want to buy time? Simple, to save money or, over time, everything changes. Perhaps the government will intervene and force the lenders to start reducing principle. Perhaps the lenders will run out of steam and they will start working with borrowers in foreclosure. So the longer you are in, the more hope you have. You can also choose to walk away by doing a short sale, a deed in lieu of foreclosure or just let the lender foreclose. But if you do a deed in lieu of foreclosure or a short sale, make sure you are not on the hook for the difference. If you defend your foreclosure, make sure you are delaying as long as you can so you can live rent free or you can stay until hopefully the market crisis will come to an end. This means the lender will perhaps finally give in to public policy and they will start creating programs and loans that will truly help a borrower to save the home. One such program would be a principle reduction. Whatever you decide, this book outlines all the options for you.

Facing Your Emotions so You Can "Fight or Flight" Your Foreclosure Tsunami

If you want to save your home, you will first have to deal with your emotions. You want to take care of this first, because your attitude is what will determine your foreclosure outcome. I once had a client who got the lock changed on him prior to the bank obtaining a judgment. The client got so upset that he just walked away from the home. He had no idea that the bank was playing mind games with him. And, rather than stand up to the bank, he gave in. That means he lost out on saving his home because of a weak mind.

I have other clients who call the lenders and tell them off and threaten the lender's staff with bodily injury. I know that foreclosure can be very personal. I know that many people are as mad as hell for being in foreclosure. And I know that banks did some horrible things to get some, not all, homeowners into this mess. However, if you want help, hold your anger for something else. You will not get far with kicking and screaming and threats to the bank. You can be sure that they will hang up the phone rather than put up with you.

What Kind of Emotions Will Be Needed to Overcome Foreclosure?

I know that when someone faces foreclosure, that person may go through a grieving process. And that is okay because the person is losing her home. Or the person may have placed some expectation on the idea of owning a home. I do know it would be best to get the grieving process out of the way. That way the person can get a fighting attitude to save the home or walk away on her own terms.

Another emotion may be revenge against the lender. I know a lot of people feel that they have been scammed into a horrible mortgage. They want to get even with the lender. This emotion will work well for you, if you decide to live rent free and defend the foreclosure. You must look out for yourself, because no one else will be doing so. Defend your home from foreclosure. As an attorney, I have noticed over the years, that my clients' fight is more plausible when their emotions are in the way. If you are mad as hell that you got this bad loan and you want to show your bank that it messed with the wrong person, then you have to put up a fight. I am not promoting physical contact. I am promoting a legal fight, which is complaining to the authorities about the bank and using the court system to handle your frustration. And you can only do so when you feel betrayed. And that is where justice comes in. You get into court, and though it takes years, you will get a judge to hear you story. And even if you lose your home in foreclosure, you are already a winner. The bank had to wait for years to get you out. This foreclosure situation reminds me of David and Goliath. Tell yourself this. You are an ordinary person and you are going to take on a billion-dollar corporation. You have had enough of corporate greed. You can no longer take being pushed around. And guess what. You sue the bank when it sues you. You force the bank to produce documents to you. You kick its ass. And you feel damn good about it. Because the banks never saw this coming. You tell your friends you are fighting your foreclosure. You get them a copy of this book. And before you know it, we have created a mental riot in this country. The government starts listening to us. Because the voices of the people are loud and clear. We decided it is time to fight back against corporate greed. And the banks are pissed because the bank, a strong lobbyist, cannot believe a person who can barely pay her mortgage can put up a hell of a fight. And then the bank has to spend money to get the home from you, because it underestimated you.

Thomas Jefferson[5] once said, "I believe that banking institutions are more dangerous to our liberties than standing armies. If the American people ever allow private banks to control the issue of their currency, first by inflation, then by deflation, the banks and corporations that will grow up around [the banks] will deprive the people of all property until their children wake-up homeless on the continent their fathers conquered. The issuing power should be taken from the banks and restored to the people, to whom it properly belongs."

The following emotions will help you fight foreclosure and save your home or walk away with no liability:

1. **Upbeat and happy**- you cannot change that foreclosure will happen to you. But you can certainly change the way you feel about it. Since foreclosure will not take your life, and you will not lose your freedom, then by all means stay happy. It is not as bad as it seems. Many people get another home after foreclosure. And you might get a much nicer one.

---

5 3rd President of the United States of America. (1743-1826)

2. **Think positively**- this goes without saying. If you think something good will come from your experience, then it will. Who knows, you might just get the house half off in terms of value.
3. **See your glass as half full.**
4. **Meditate**- this will help you to stay present. Avoid the mind wondering on what could go wrong. And the horrific stories that people make up or the bank paying actors to put on television to scare you into thinking that foreclosure means you are living in hell. When you meditate, you will stay present and that is the only thing that matters in life. The here and now.
5. **Exercise**- this is good for your health. But it will also help you to reduce the stress and anxiety associated with being in foreclosure.
6. **Strategic thinking**- Now is the time to start thinking how your foreclosure situation can benefit you. You should be reading this book over and over again. It is full of information that can help you. You should also read the paper and go on the internet for information. Many bloggers are beginning to talk about the borrowers that are gaming the bank and living rent free. And it appears that those borrowers will be doing that for years to come, which means plenty of money in their pocket. After all, they just created their own stimulus package. Those borrowers understand an opportunity when they see one. And whether it is right or wrong, it won't matter 100 years from today. If fact, my opinion on that is perhaps if borrowers were not living rent free, the recession would be a lot worse. Imagine now that if they are not paying a mortgage, the money is still going somewhere. It is perhaps going to vacations, restaurants, new cars, start up a business, college funds for your children, your retirement or whenever it is going; it is going back into the economy, which is a good thing for the economy.
7. **Hopeful**- Hope is a good thing. It is a great feeling to know that through your trial, something good will come of it. So be hopeful. Some of my clients just delay their

foreclosure with the anticipation of hope. They figure at some point, maybe the government will step in and start ordering the banks to reduce the value of the home. Some even delay it for a few months, until they obtain a job. Once they get a job, then they can start paying their mortgages again. So when you are hopeful, you will fight.

8. **Patience**- The foreclosure process may be long. It may take months. It may take years. It may take weeks to get a response for a letter that was written to your lender. So it would help if you are a patient person. And you are not looking for an overnight fix. I can't emphasize how many letters and phone calls must be made to the lender to get a response. And to get the response that you need. I have so many clients calling and telling me off, because they think I am not doing my job. Then after six months go by, they get a response and then they are happy. I keep telling the clients, to just be patient. But we live in a generation where everyone wants a quick fix. There will never be a quick fix to the foreclosure crisis. So you had better learn to be patient. Things will work out for you. How do you feel when you are getting frustrated over not hearing from the lender and then you raise your blood pressure. You add stress to your life. You take it out on your spouse and children and then after six months, the lender gives you the modification. Was that stress really worth it? It is silly to stress when you do not even know if you will get approved or denied.

These emotions tend to work against a borrower who tries to save her home from foreclosure:

1. **Angry or hostile**- if you are too angry about your situation, you will not be able to obtain the help you need. Anger and hostility repel most people. Calling a lender and threatening it with bodily harm will not get you the results you are looking for. In fact, the lender may even be that much more eager to contact its foreclosure attorney with a little note that says: "make a rush on this one." All of a sudden, you would recognize that nothing will be going your way.

2. **Anxious and edgy**- you must live in present moment. Being anxious only produces stress and negative energy. What if you happen to get on the phone with the lender and the lender can sense that you are anxious. The lender may use that as an opportunity to charge you extra fees, because it recognizes in your voice that anything may go.

3. **Frustrated**- a person who gets dissatisfied in a short period of time, will not get too far with overcoming her foreclosure crisis.

4. **Victim mentality**- this is a person who thinks only bad things will happen to her.

5. **Helpless**- a person who believes that the world is against her.

6. **Proud**- people with pride will not seek help because they are too embarrassed to be in the position. Unfortunately, there is nothing prideful in foreclosure. Losses happen in life. If it is not foreclosure, it could be the death of a loved one. It could be an illness. It could be a divorce, a job. It will be something else for sure.

7. **Negativity and pessimism**- if you say it will not work for you, then guess what, it won't.

8. **Moral conviction**- I have many lawyers and borrowers who refuse to work with my Firm because they think that people should not defend foreclosure or they should not attempt to save their home. These lawyers

and borrowers believe that we all have a moral obligation to pay our mortgage loan, even if the bank
tricks you in obtaining the loan. And if we cannot pay,
then we have a moral obligation to leave without putting up a defense. Because of their moral convictions, I
cannot convince them that foreclosure defense is their
answer. As such, my Firm will not able to defend them
in foreclosure. If you too have a moral conviction, if
foreclosure defenses feel wrong to you, then you perhaps will have to lose your home. If you feel guilty living
rent free, then foreclosure defense will not work for you.
Let me tell you a little secret. Do you know who is telling
you that foreclosure defense is not right? Your greedy
bank, who pays millions if not billions of dollars to ad-
vertise on brain washing you and your children into doing what they want you to do. And I hope someday
you will recognize that morality is a personal opinion
that you agree to accept. The banks only want your
money and they will play mind games to get it. One
of those games happens to be their moral convictions
that you choose to accept.

9. **Naive**- Some borrowers do not understand what is happening to them. Some feel very naive, or they think
that somehow it will work out. Others do a stupid thing.
They call the lender to ask for advice on whether they
should hire an attorney to keep them in the home.
Of course, the lender convinces the borrower not to.
Why? Because it is not in the lender's best interest. And
of course, the lender does not tell that to the borrower.
Instead, the lender convinces the borrower to trust the
lender and that everything will be fine. The borrowers
believe the lender and within a matter of three months,
the lender kicks the borrower out of the home, through
foreclosure. Would you call your enemy for advice?
Do you know the relationship that you, a borrower, has
with a lender? It is called creditor and debtor. I do not
care if you hang out with the branch manager. I do
not care if everyone at your local bank knows you by
first name. They know what your favorite meal is and

they send you a birthday card every year to wish you happy birthday. You are just a debtor and the bank wants your money. If you see things the way they are, you will have a more positive experience.

10. **Weak**- I am not talking about someone who is physically fragile. I am talking about someone who has a weak mind. This person gives up too quickly. This person cannot handle mind games. This person does not like to get involved with disputes. This person refuses to fight.

11. **Desperate**- something people are very desperate to get out of is the foreclosure situation, because they are not comfortable with the uncertain. The lenders can see that. Therefore, the lender takes advantage of them. I have seen the lender reduce payments by $100.00 per month and, on top of that, the modification says that the borrower waives all rights to raise affirmative defenses or counterclaims. That is not a wise position to be in. Remember the golden rule. You are a debtor and the bank is a creditor. The bank is only looking out for its best interests, and not yours. If you benefit the bank in any way, then for sure, it will extend some form of help to you. If you do not benefit the bank, then there will be no help.

Overview of Foreclosure

A foreclosure is a legal process used by a lender if the homeowner fails to make mortgage payments as the lender and homeowner agreed they would. There are basically two types of foreclosure. They are judicial and non-judicial foreclosures.

A judicial foreclosure involves the sale of the mortgaged property under the supervision of the court. The proceeds from the sale of the property will be given first to satisfy the first lien holder and, if any proceeds are left, they go to the junior lien holder and then to the borrower.

Chapter 1
Understanding Judicial and
Non-Judicial Foreclosures

In the United States of America, if someone is going through foreclosure, then it will either be facing a judicial foreclosure or a non-judicial foreclosure. A judicial or non-judicial foreclosure has to do with the state where the homeowner lives. A judicial foreclosure is conducted through a court system, where a non-judicial foreclosure isn't.

What Is a Judicial Foreclosure Sale?
A judicial foreclosure is conducted through a court system. The State Statutes outline whether the state is a judicial or non-judicial state.

How Does It Work?
Once the borrower misses at least three mortgage payments, the lender will then send a Notice of Default letter to the borrower.

Notice of Default letter
That letter will tell the borrower that she missed a payment and if she refuses to cure the default, then the lender will accelerate the loan and the note, which means the lender is about to initiate foreclosure. It will then give the borrower 30 days to cure the default. It will also inform the borrower that if the default is not cured within 30 days, the lender

will be forwarding the borrower's information to the lender's foreclosure attorney. If the borrower fails to cure the default within 30 days, the lender's attorney will then start the foreclosure proceedings. So the next step would be the lender's attorney, after the 30 days expire, but no sooner,[6] will prepare and file a Lis Pendens (which is attached to the property) and a complaint against the borrower.

The Lis Pendens
The Lis Pendens gets recorded in the public records where the property that is subject to foreclosure is located. A Lis Pendens clouds the title by placing the world on notice that the property is subject to a foreclosure action by the borrower's lender. The Lis Pendens will have the style of the case and the legal description of the property.

The Complaint
The complaint will be served upon the borrower by a sheriff or a process server. The borrower will have 20 calendar days from the date she receives the complaint to respond to the lawsuit. In the bank's complaint, it will state that the borrower is being sued by the lender, and the action is a foreclosure action. The bank will then outline the facts. It will talk about the amount of money owed, the date and year the borrower took out the loan, the last time payment was made, and the fact that a default occurred because the borrower failed to pay. It will then request that the judge order the sale of the property by granting summary judgment.

Summary Judgment
Once summary judgment is granted in favor of the bank, the property will usually be sold after 30 days from the date a publication of notice has been placed in circulation.[7] The sale will be a public action and the successful bidder will obtain a certificate of title after the sale has been completed.

---

6 State Statute may vary, so check your State Statute for clarity.

7 However, each State may vary. It would be wise to check your State Statute, as the above information is in reference to a Judicial Sale in the State of Florida.

Certificate of Title

Once the certificate of title is issued, that will give the new owner title to the property. It could be the bank or it could be a third party who went to foreclosure auction to bid on the property. After the certificate of title is issued, the new owner will perhaps request a writ of possession to be issued. If the borrower does not leave the foreclosed home the date the certificate of title is issued, the new owner (who obtained title to the property) will start an eviction process. Once the sale is granted, the judge also gave orders to issue a writ of possession to the successful bidder. That writ gives the new owner physical possession of the property. At times a writ will be enforced through an eviction process because it gives a local sheriff the power from the judge to place the new owner of the property in physical control of the property. So if the owner does not leave the property, then the new owner will initiate an eviction process. The new owner will then hand over the writ of possession to a local sheriff and the sheriff will post it on the premises. That will give the borrower 24 hours to vacate the premises. If not, then the sheriff will physically remove the borrower from the premises, as the borrower is no longer the owner of the property.

What Is a Non-Judicial Foreclosure Sale?

A non-judicial foreclosure will vary from state to state because the State Statutes outline what will be required. For example, in some states, a Notice of Default must be issued. Other states may require only a Notice of Sale. Other states may require only a publication for the Notice of Sale to announce the sale. It would be wise to review your state's statutes as they will for sure tell you how the non-judicial sale is being conducted by your state.

Deed in Trust

It is also important to note that if you obtain a deed in trust, then for sure that would be a non-judicial foreclosure sale. If you obtain a mortgage, then the lender may choose a non-judicial foreclosure sale, if the state allows that. If you obtain a mortgage and you reside in a judicial sale state, then for sure it would be done through the court system.

Power of Sale Clause

In a non-judicial foreclosure state, the power of sale clause is used by the lender to force the sale. The lender does not need the court to force sale because of the power of sale clause, which has been contracted by the borrower and the lender.

The table shows which state follows, judicial, non-judicial or both.

State[8]	Judicial	Non-Judicial
Alabama	•	•
Alaska	•	•
Arizona	•	•
Arkansas	•	•
California	•	•
Colorado	•	•
Connecticut	•	
Delaware	•	
District of Columbia		•
Florida	•	
Georgia	•	•

8 As you can tell from the chart, there are some states that recognize both judicial and non judicial sale. However, check your State Statute since researching for this book comes with brevity. If there is any discrepancy with the chart and your State Statute, then consider your State Statute to be the governing authority.

Hawaii	•	•
Idaho	•	•
Illinois	•	
Indiana	•	
Iowa	•	•
Kansas	•	
Kentucky	•	
Louisiana	•	
Maine	•	
Maryland	•	
Massachusetts	•	
Michigan		•
Minnesota	•	•
Mississippi	•	•
Missouri	•	•
Montana	•	•
Nebraska	•	
Nevada	•	•
New Hampshire		•
New Jersey	•	

New Mexico	•	
New York	•	
North Carolina	•	•
North Dakota	•	
Ohio	•	
Oklahoma	•	•
Oregon	•	•
Pennsylvania	•	
Rhode Island	•	•
South Carolina	•	
South Dakota	•	•
Tennessee		•
Texas	•	•
Utah	•	•
Vermont	•	
Virginia	•	•
Washington	•	•
West Virginia		•
Wisconsin	•	•
Wyoming	•	•

What are the major differences between Judicial vs. Non Judicial?

Judicial	Non Judicial
Lender has less control	Lender has more control[9]
court order	non court order
slower for lender	faster for lender
Sale order by a judge or the court	The trustee orders or administrate the sale[10]
more legal fees	fewer legal fees

9 The Lender has more control over this foreclosure situation, because there is no court system involved. As such, the borrower cannot raise legal defenses and the borrower cannot be heard in front of a judge or a jury, that would otherwise show mercy to a borrower. Some legal defenses raised in foreclosure would even throw a foreclosure case out and the lender will not be able to foreclosure on the property. Non-judicial states do not provide this leeway.

10 This trustee must not be confused with a United States Trustee in Bankruptcy. Just keep in mind, if you are in a non-judicial foreclosure, then become familiar with the term trustee. For more on the non-judicial foreclosure, check your state Statute which will outline the foreclosure process.

Chapter 2
Obtaining a Loan Modification to Save Your Home from Foreclosure

What Is a Loan Modification?

A loan modification is when the lender makes your mortgage payment lower because you cannot afford the current mortgage payment on your home. In order to qualify for the loan modification, you must let the lender know that you cannot pay the mortgage you have now because you are suffering some form of hardship like a loss of job, divorce, or illness.

> **HELPFUL HINT**-*the only hardship that the lender will accept is economic loss (which include job loss or decrease in pay) divorce or health issues (by you or a loved one) or death of a loved one. So make sure yours fall into one of those categories.*

Documents Required for Modification:

The following documents are generally required from a homeowner to obtain a modification:

1. Last 2 years of tax returns.
2. 3 Months of your recent bank statements.
3. A hardship letter (see appendix for sample of hardship letters).
4. 4506 T (lender provides it. See also http://www.irstaxrecords.com/4506.pdf for a sample of one).
5. Lenders application (lender provides it).

6. Proof of homeowners insurance if it is not escrowed.
7. Proof of property taxes being paid if it is not escrowed.
8. Profit and Loss Statement if you are self-employed.
9. Driver's Licenses.
10. Utility bill (which reflects that you reside at the premises).

How Do You Qualify for a Loan Modification?

In order to qualify for a loan modification the borrower must meet the following criteria:

1. Primary residence.
2. Existing 1st mortgage of $729,750 or less.
3. Mortgage issued prior to January 1, 2009.
4. Your current mortgage expense is not greater than 31% of your gross income.

A Payment Reduction Estimator will show you to come up with the 31%. For more information visit the web page makinghomeaffordable.gov.

Myths about Loan Modification:

1. **You need good credit to obtain one.** Good credit is not a factor in obtaining a loan modification. The lender anticipated that a person who is obtaining a loan modification must be having financial troubles. One sign of financial struggle is bad credit, since the borrower will rob from Peter to pay Paul. As such, the person's credit cannot be that great. If it were, then that would defeat the purpose of helping homeowners in foreclosure to save the home. I have heard that people with credit score of under 450 obtain loan modifications.
2. **You can modify your payment as many times as you want.** With this foreclosure crisis, many investors or strategy borrowers or borrowers that love a free ride can sense that the banking system is having a financial meltdown.

They know about the court system being back logged with foreclosure and they are just having a good time not paying their mortgage. When the modification was first introduced, there were not much restrictions on it. It was a new product. So the free riders would just keep applying for modification and then they would just stop paying. Then the bank would keep putting them into foreclosure and then take them out of foreclosure. These borrowers did it for a while and then the bank caught on to their game. As such, a recent law passed that a loan modification can only be done two times for the life of the loan. So if you are planning on pulling a fast one by reapplying more than two times, be warned. You are skating on thin ice.

3. **It is a very easy process.** Modification is not an easy process. And it does not look like it will ever be an easy process. You are required to document your income. You are required to sign extensive documents. And you will be calling and following up until your face turns blue, brown or grey or whatever color it changes to when you become angry or frustrated. You will have your work cut out for you. No doubt. You will never hear anyone say that they had the time of their life obtaining a modification and they can't wait to do it again. It appears that the lender and the government are working to correct this issue. But let me just give you the logic in this. Why on earth would a bank reward someone who is in foreclosure? Then what incentive would borrowers have to pay for their homes? As such, the process will always be difficult because the bank is trying to tell us something. They are trying to tell us not to go into foreclosure. And so they are punishing the borrowers' behavior. If the process is easy, then rest assured, there will be plenty strategic foreclosures going on. The modification process will be long. Even if you qualify, expect a waiting time of around six months or more.

Different Types of Loan Modifications

FHA Home Affordable (HAMP)

This program was announced sometime in March, 2010. So do not be surprised if you do not hear too much about it. The program was designed by the Obama Administration to make sure that owners with FHA loans obtain an opportunity to save their home, through a modification, which would equate to cheaper payments.

Eligibility

1. Home must be your primary residence.
2. The loan is an FHA loan (insured by FHA).
3. You have made at least 4 payments under the loan.
4. Your monthly mortgage payment exceeds 31% of your gross income.
5. You cannot pay the current mortgage on your home, due to some form of hardship.
6. You can only do this program once. So if you are doing a second try at the FHA HAMP, you will not obtain the modification.
7. The unpaid principle is less than $729,500.00.
8. You must be delinquent on the mortgage for at least 30 days.

A.   HAMP Loan Modification

A HAMP modification only applies to borrowers whose loan is owned by Fannie Mae or Freddie Mac. The reason behind that is the Obama administration can only bail out loans that are federally funded or under federal guarantee. So a homeowner will not be receiving a HAMP loan if the property is not owned by Fannie Mae or Freddie Mac or any type or form of government-backed loan. You may be asking how on earth will you know if your property is owned by Fannie Mae or Freddie Mac? Simple, you can go on Fannie Mae and Fredie Mac web page. They are http://www.fanniemae.com/loanlookup/ and https://ww3.freddiemac.com/corporate/.

Put your property address in and it will come up on whether Fannie Mae or Freddie Mac owns the loan. If they do, then your lender will extend the HAMP modification to you when you call your lender. If the property is not owned by Fannie Mae or Freddie Mac, not to worry, there are other non-HAMP modifications out there.

How Is the HAMP Calculated?

You will need to know how HAMP is calculated for a few reasons. First, you can predetermine whether or not you will be approved. It is very important that you attempt to pre-approve yourself without the lender doing so at first. Some clients have worked a second job, just to get the modification. If they had sent in the paperwork with only one job, they would never have saved their home. So if there is something that you can do, legally, to help get the modification, then do so. So try to learn how it is calculated to see how you can maximize your opportunity to obtain one. The lender will do a simple calculation. The lender will calculate your new mortgage payment to be no more than 31% of your gross income. Suppose you make $3000.00 per month, before taxes are taken out. If the lender will extend a HAMP program to you, then the lender will come up with a plan in which your principle, interest and taxes, and insurance and maintenance fee (if applicable) will be no more than $930.00. How did I get this number? If your gross income is $3000.00, then multiple that by 31%.

Will the Lender Consider My Debt Under the HAMP Program?

Most people think that they will not qualify for HAMP because their debt exceeds their income. Again, the HAMP program is not designed to consider the homeowner's debt. The reason behind this is simple.

The lender already calculated that if the homeowner is really serious about saving her home, the homeowner will change her priorities by cutting out other debt, so she can pay her mortgage payment. So the only calculation that the lender uses is to get the borrower's mortgage not to exceed 31% of the borrower's gross income.

B.   A Non-HAMP Modification

If you do not qualify for HAMP because your property is not owned by Fannie Mae or Freddie Mac, or the lender chooses not to extend it to you for other reasons, then don't give up. (By the way, the lender has sole discretion of denying it to you and I have seen letters with vague explanation). In any event, you may qualify for a non-HAMP modification. This too will have the effect of providing you with cheaper mortgage payments by either reducing the principle, interest or both. You will still need to provide the additional documentation, and then you might have additional qualification.

Will My Debt to Income Ratio Matter in a Non-HAMP Modification?

It may. Since the government does not have any power over the non-HAMP, then lenders and investors who owned these mortgages will work with the borrowers in developing a non-HAMP modification. However, it may be a lot stickier because the lenders may consider the borrower's debt to income ratio. Or the lender may require from the borrower additional paperwork such as an explanation of certain credit history.

HELPFUL HINT- *if you find out that your loan is not owned by Fannie Mae or Freddie Mac, then clean up your debt to income ratio before applying for the non-HAMP. That way, you maximize your chances of obtaining it. One way you can clean up your debt* *to income ratio is by reducing your debt or increasing your income.*

Drawbacks of Non-HAMP

Because the non-HAMP is not governed by the government, the servicer, or the investor (who owns the note) gets to make the decision. For a non-HAMP, the investor or servicer may require the homeowner to pay up front fees. Homeowners may end up paying over $5000.00 to obtain the non-HAMP program. A homeowner may end up paying the upfront fee and still gets denied the non-HAMP program. The thing of it all is that the investors and servicer get to make the rules, and most of it is to make a profit for them. But don't get discouraged, just approach it with caution. If the investor feels that the non-HAMP payment proposed will make them a profit, then it will be likely that the non-HAMP modification will work out for you. Whatever is in the servicer's or investor's best interest is what you will obtain.

Chapter 3
Redeeming Your Property to Save Your Home

Tonya Brown lives in a judicial state, the state of Florida. She owns her home there. Tonya Brown faced foreclosure and her home got sold at the public auction. Tonya, however, came up with sufficient funds a few days after foreclosure to save the home. Tonya contacted a foreclosure attorney who helped her file the proper paper work with the court. Tonya saved her home from foreclosure, as Tonya exercised the Right of Redemption even though the house was sold at the public auction. So now that I have explained that scenario, what is the Right of Redemption? Below is an explanation of what it is and how it works.

What Is the Right of Redemption and How Does it Work?
Under a Right of Redemption, a homeowner will be able to buy his property back from the person who bought it at a foreclosure. A right for redemption is set by state statute and is not in a mortgage clause. Therefore, in order for a troubled borrower to redeem his property, he must be in a state that recognizes the Right of Redemption. Right to Redemption usually occurs in states for which foreclosure is a judicial proceeding. Therefore, if a state is a non-judicial foreclosure state, then there will be no Right of Redemption. Each state statute may vary on the time period allowed to redeem the property. In the state of Florida, the Right of Redemption occurs up to 11 days before the certificate of title is issued. Under Florida law, once the certificate of title

is issued, then the borrower can no longer save her property. In Florida, a certificate of title is issued 11 days after the date the property is sold at the public auction. So, in order for a homeowner to redeem her property, the homeowner has until the date the certificate of title is issued. There is very little to be done after the title is issued and the homeowner loses her right to redeem the property. If the property is sold to a third party at the foreclosure auction, under the state statue, the third party will have to give the homeowner an opportunity to redeem the property, so the third party will technically not be the owner until the certificate of title is issued. Third parties really do not own the properties that they purchased at the foreclosure public auction until the Right of Redemption expires. It is not uncommon for investors to purchase properties at the foreclosure public auction but not move forward on renovating the homes or evicting a troubled borrower who would be in the house, until the date the certificate of title is issued. These investors know from experience that any homeowner can save his home even after the property is sold at a public auction.

Right of Redemption Time Pursuant to Statutory Period
California is a state that follows the Right of Redemption rule. But under California law the Right of Redemption occurs in as little as three months and as much as 12 months. It varies, because if the property sold has surplus, then the period to redeem the property is less than 12 months. A surplus means when a foreclosure property is sold, the borrower will make money as it is sold for a lot more than the mortgage amount. In most judicial states, including Florida, a Right of Redemption will be extended if the borrower can show that some form of fraud, or egregious mistake occurred during the foreclosure proceeding or sale. If a borrower suspects that fraud occurred in her foreclosure, it would be wise for her to contact a foreclosure attorney who will be able to mount a defense for getting back the property. Remember, foreclosure attorneys are experts that handle foreclosure and perhaps know more about maneuvering the law in the borrower's favor. A home is an important

asset to a borrower, so she should hire experts who can help her save her home.

Explanation of Right of Redemption and the Difference between Right of Redemption and Right of Reinstatement

At times, homeowners may contact their lenders to see how they can make good on a defaulted mortgage. As you can tell from reading this book, there are many options available to a troubled borrower. Basically, if a borrower wants to save her home from foreclosure, there will be plenty of opportunity. However, it is very important that the homeowner understands the different stages of foreclosure, because what opportunity may be available for the homeowner may depend on the stage of the foreclosure process. For instance, a Right of Redemption is usually available after the property is foreclosed upon. And as such, it would be silly for a homeowner to contact the lender when the homeowner is 45 days late on the payment and request to redeem the property. It won't happen, because that would be the wrong stage during which to request a redemption. Also, it appears that lenders will not fully explain to homeowners their right to redeem the property after the property is foreclosed. Perhaps this could be because a lender does not want to promote buyers waiting for last minute to save their home. Or it just does not make good business sense to have homeowners default on their loans and then save their homes even though they went into foreclosure. Who knows? What I can tell you is that the more knowledge you have about foreclosure, the better. You will tackle your foreclosure situation with calm, and you will come out with the result that you need.

Day 1: Tonya Brown purchased a home in 2005. In January, 2006, Tonya Brown missed her first mortgage payment. She was 30 days late. Nothing happened. In fact, she received a letter from her lender advising her that she was 30 days past due and it will report her late payment to the credit bureau. Tonya still does not make a payment. After **Day 91**, Tonya still does not make a payment.

Finally, Tonya receives a Notice of Default letter from her lender. It threatens her with legal action. It advises her to make her three payments, along with interest and late fees. If she refuses to do so, it advised her that she would be referred to the lender's attorney and she would be facing foreclosure. Tonya still does not make a payment. **Day 135**: Tonya wakes up to a loud knock on her door. It is the town's sheriff. He asks her if she is Tonya Brown. She responds yes. He hands her some paper work and says, "You have been served." Tonya Brown accepts the paper work and it reads that she has 20 days to respond. Tonya Brown still does nothing. Because of the backlog in the state of Florida, Tonya receives from the lender six months after that complaint a Motion for Summary Judgment. Tonya contacted the lender and asks what she can do to save the home. The lender asks a few questions and explains to her that she could reinstate her mortgage. The lender explains to Tonya that reinstatement means that if Tonya pays the current mortgage and the arrears in full along with the interest, late fees, title search and attorney fees and all the costs, the lender would dismiss the lawsuit. The lender would discharge the Lis Pendens and Tonya would again be out of foreclosure. The total amount Tonya would have to come up with would be around $12,395.00. The lender calculates the reinstatement as follows. She has not made a payment since January 2006. It has been over nine months since Tonya has been in foreclosure. Therefore, Tonya would have to pay the mortgage payment for nine months in one lump sum, along with the late fees for nine months, title search and attorney fees. Tonya accepts the reinstatement verbally. But something happens and Tonya just does not show up with the money to reinstate the mortgage. Finally, during the Summary Judgment hearing, Tonya's lender obtains a favorable judge who grants the lender the permission to sell the home 90 days after publication. Tonya receives the information regarding the notice of sale, as the standard requirement is for the lender to copy Tonya and any defaulted borrower on the paper work that it sends to the court. Tonya again calls the lender and it still offers her a reinstatement, even though it has a date to sell the home. Of course, more fees and costs are added to the balance. Tonya still does nothing. Within two days of the property being sold, Tonya contacts the lender, who advises her it owns the home because it received title at the public auction. Tonya quickly hired a foreclosure attorney, who helped to get her home back. The foreclosure attorney contacts the lender and advises the lender of the statutory period of the right to redeem the home. The lender comes up with some figures that Tonya can live with, and Tonya pays the lender the full amount. **Last day:** Tonya saved her home from foreclosure in the redemption statutory period.

Right of Redemption versus Reinstatement of a Mortgage

Right of Redemption
1. It is statutory and not by contract.

2. The buyer can exercise the Right of Redemption after the property is sold at a foreclosure auction but before the certificate of title is issued.

3. It cannot be used during the foreclosure proceeding.

4. It can only be used after the sale of the property occurs.

Reinstatement of Mortgage
1. It is by contract and not statutory.

2. It cannot be used after the property is sold at the public auction, but prior to the sale date.

3. The buyer must pay all the delinquent accounts, with interest, late fees, court costs, attorney fees and title search if applicable.

Chapter 4
Avoiding Foreclosure through Forbearance

What Is a Forbearance?
A forbearance is an agreement in which the lender agrees to stop the mortgage installments that the borrower has to meet monthly. Therefore, the borrower avoids making a few mortgage payments. A forbearance is only a temporary fix. At some point, the borrower will have to get back on making the mortgage payments. A forbearance generally last for less than six months. However, I have seen cases where the lenders in certain situations extend the forbearance longer than the six months. If a borrower obtains a forbearance, then she would avoid foreclosure, because the lender would agree for the borrower to miss payments.

How Must a Borrower Qualify for a Forbearance?

Missed Payment
In order to obtain a forbearance, the borrower must first contact the lender before a payment is missed. However, I have seen were the lender has placed the borrower in forbearance after a few missed payments. But it would generally be wise for the borrower to contact the lender before a missed payment.

Borrower Faces a Financial Hardship
In order to obtain a forbearance, a borrower must convince the lender that the borrower is facing some temporary

financial problems. The lender will generally request that the borrower prove that he can make the reduced payment plan, and he must qualify for that new payment plan. Once the forbearance ends, the borrower goes back to making the regular mortgage payments. However, there will be a little extra amount that will be added to the balance. That amount represents the non-payment of the mortgage interest or the difference with the reduce amount. The repayment will not exceed a year. Forbearance, in a nut shell, just allows the borrower to pay the loan amount that he owes over a longer period of time.

How Will You Know if Forbearance Is Right for You?

1. **You fall under the hardship** If you fall under the hardship that the lender outlines, then perhaps a forbearance would be right for you. A forbearance will for sure allow you to not be into foreclosure. So this may be a very easy option because you avoid foreclosure altogether, which means you get to save your home.
2. **The lender qualifies you** If you meet the guidelines under the forbearance, then that may be a sign that the forbearance may be right for you. If the lender says you qualify under the program, then maybe you should really consider the forbearance.
3. **You will be able to meet the agreement that the lender outlines** The lender is going to come up with a new payment, temporarily. So your old mortgage payment will no longer be in effect. The temporary payment may start off very little amount. However, the second payment, when the lender tacks on the old debt to your mortgage, may be a little higher than your regular payment. It would be wise for you to really calculate if you can make such payment. Because if you fail to meet the payments, then you will fall into foreclosure.
4. **When the Forbearance ends, you will be able to pay the mortgage payment** Once your forbearance ends, then the regular mortgage payment (the one that you had prior to the forbearance) kicks in. That means you will

be back to where you were prior to the forbearance. Here is an example: Adam Brown is a 35-year-old borrower in the state of Florida. Adam recently lost his job, which caused him not to be able make his mortgage payment. His monthly mortgage payment is $1500.00 per month. Adam contacted his lender and submitted the proper paperwork and the lender gave Adam a forbearance. The forbearance agreement does not allow Adam to pay on his mortgage for six months. The lender agreed to the forbearance for Adam in March 2009. Adam will not have a mortgage payment for April 2009, May 2009, June 2009, July 2009 and August 2009. What happened to those payments? The lender suspended the mortgage for six months, which caused Adam to work out his hardship, find a job and get back on track. However, the interest that occurred for the last six months does not go away. The lender either tacked it back onto the loan, or the lender will extend Adam's loan year for an additional six months. So Adam will pay for it at some point. Once the six months expire, Adam is again required to pay on the mortgage. If the lender did not agree to have Adam catch up the six months over the next year, but it agreed to tack it on the back, then Adam will go back to $1500.00 per month. If the lender and Adam agree that the six months of interest must be paid over 12 months, then Adam will pay a higher amount for 12 months, and once Adam catches up the back amount, then he will go back to his regular $1500.00 per month payment. So keep in mind, this will only benefit a borrower whose temporary hardship will leave him back in the position he was, had there not been a hardship. If a borrower's income is lower or the borrower is working part time rather than full time, then the forbearance won't work, because the borrower will not be able to afford the mortgage payment once the forbearance expires. However, if a borrower is hopeful, then the borrower should go for it. At least the borrower bought six extra months.

5. **Your hardship is truly temporary** It appears to me as a foreclosure attorney, that there seem to be two type of people that are applying for forbearance. The first one has to do with a troubled borrower who really has not seen that she cannot afford the mortgage to begin with. This borrower will be hopeful and very speculative. This borrower obtained a home through the bank's stupidity since the bank was giving everyone a mortgage. And the homeowner does not have the income to sustain the mortgage payment. The homeowner just cannot face the reality and the writing on the wall that she may have overextended herself in purchasing the home. The homeowner may have done well in the past, but because of the previous recession her income has been reduced, but she is still hopeful that she will be able to make big money soon. As such, this homeowner will perhaps get involved with a forbearance because the homeowner is betting that a big job is around the corner. Those forbearances will never work. The homeowner will soon lose the home, because the income is not enough to sustain the mortgage. However, because life is a free enterprise and people can do whatever they want, the homeowner is free to pursue an unrealistic dream and expectation.

The second type of person applying for a forbearance tends to be a borrower that truly hit a hard rock and the issue will be resolved quickly. This includes a pregnant woman who took time off from work to have her baby. Her employer does not pay her for time off for pregnancy, but she still has the same income coming to her once she gets back to work. Under that situation, the forbearance will work because she will go back to the same income. Another type of person that I see to be very successful in forbearance is a sale person who makes big commission. Sales people might have a dry spell for a while, but they have so much pending commission in the pipeline that once they close on their sales, they will be funded. This could be a realtor, an insurance adjuster, and just about anyone whose job involves sales, and there are pending prospects.

6. **You accept that you cannot afford the home, but you are doing a forbearance just to buy time** What if you have finally come to peace with the fact that you made a mistake. You purchased a home that you cannot afford. But you decide to do what millions of people are doing, live rent free. If that is the case, then the next option will be to obtain a forbearance. That way, you are not put into foreclosure right away. But you will buy precious time. Again, let me give you the biggest reason people buy time--to save money and to make up the loss of purchasing a bad investment. If you can convince your lender to forbear your loan because things will get better for you in the future, then by all means do it. If the lender is dumb enough to give you the break, then count yourself lucky. A lot of people would love to have it. And if you are clever to talk people into things, then you can surely save some money. I have seen, over the years, so many homeowners not getting the big picture. I have had homeowners just walk away from the home, because they said it was just stupid to live in a foreclosure property rent free. You have got to understand this. Your biggest investment is your home. If the government says most people spend 31% of their gross income on a mortgage, think about how much you can save for six months without a mortgage payment. But other homeowners have told me that it was too painful for them to stay in a house they will lose. They just felt like staying in the home and getting attached to it, was a lose-lose situation because they were delaying a very painful situation. I want to compare it to a person on death row. They know they are going to die, but they still have their attorneys file appeals because they would rather live a few more years, than a smaller year. And besides, this home thing is a business for the bank. Maybe homeowners need to see staying and saving money as a business venture.

When a Forbearance Will Not Work for the Borrower:

Forbearance will not be right for you if:

1. Your income has been reduced substantially.
2. You went from a full time job to a part time job.
3. You are at the verge of bankruptcy.
4. You overpaid for your home and you are being wiped out by paying the mortgage.
5. You have to borrow from your retirement, savings, credit cards and friends and family to pay for your mortgage.
6. You will not be able to afford the new mortgage payment that the lender proposed once the forbearance expires.
7. You can barely afford the mortgage payment now.
8. You know that foreclosure is the only way you can get out of the loan.
9. You cannot sleep at night because you are worried how you will make your mortgage payment.
10. You bought the home to keep up with the Joneses.
11. You are underwater with the property and you refuse to let the property go because you are emotionally attached to it.
12. Professionals who you talk to about your loan issue suggest to you to let the property go or to do a loan modification.
13. You do not feel that forbearance is right for you.
14. You stay up at night hoping for things to get better.
15. The lender pressured you to obtain the forbearance and you do not see any benefit to it.
16. Your mortgage exceeds the value of your home by more than 50%.
17. Your lifestyle has changed tremendously that you are allocating your mortgage payment to care for family members, health issues or divorce.
18. You purchased your home at the wrong time– your purchased your home when the property values were inflated.
19. You have more than one mortgage on your property.
20. You are overextended.

Chapter 5
Filing for Chapter 7 and Chapter 13 Bankruptcy Protection to Save Your Home

Chapter 7 and Chapter 13 to Save Your Home or Stall Foreclosure

If you are a homeowner facing foreclosure, you can save your home or stall the foreclosure process by filing for Chapter 7 bankruptcy petition. Even though this book is limited to foreclosure defense, it will outline how Chapter 7 and chapter 13 bankruptcy can help you.[11] These bankruptcies can be a tool in helping a homeowner save her home from foreclosure.

What Is Chapter 7 Bankruptcy?

Chapter 7 is a liquidation form of bankruptcy. It allows the debtor to wipe out all unsecured debt, including credit cards, payday loans, judgments, and medical bills. Chapter 7 is often considered a fresh start because the debtor gets a clean slate when all of his unsecured debt is wiped out. For purposes of this book, we will focus on how chapter 7 can help the homeowner save her home from being brought into foreclosure. When a debtor files for chapter 7 bankruptcy protection, the date the bankruptcy case gets filed, the debtor obtains a case number and an automatic stay from the federal court.

---

11 Bankruptcy will stop all action against a borrower regardless of whether or not the property subject to foreclosure is a judicial or non-judicial state.

What Is Chapter 13 Bankruptcy?

Chapter 13 bankruptcy means that the debtor (person who files for bankruptcy) decided she wants to repay some or all her creditors with a better payment plan. This includes a better interest rate, or no interest rate at all. However, a person who chooses to file chapter 13 must have a steady income, since chapter 13 requires a payment plan.

What Is an Automatic Stay and What Does It Do; and Would Chapters 7 and 13 give a Borrower an Automatic Stay?

Once you file for a chapter 7 or chapter 13 bankruptcy petition, a debtor obtains an automatic stay. With the automatic stay, the U.S. Clerk will notify all the creditors listed on the paper work that the debtor filed for bankruptcy protection. If not, then either the debtor or the debtor's attorney will file a suggestion of bankruptcy with the state court where all the pending lawsuits against the debtor are filed.[12] The suggestion of bankruptcy informs the creditor to stop all collection activities against the debtor. So, let us say, Ann Brown is in foreclosure. The bank obtained a sale date for her property and the property will be sold at a public auction on January 10, 2010. Ann immediately seeks bankruptcy protection by filing for chapter 7 or chapter 13 (depending upon which type of bankruptcy Ann wishes to pursue). She files bankruptcy on January 2, 2010. At that point, Ann will prepare and file a suggestion of bankruptcy with the state court that has the pending foreclosure property. Ann saved her home from foreclosure as the sale gets cancelled because Ann sought bankruptcy protection prior to the sale date. If Ann did not file for bankruptcy protection, then the sale would have gone through and Ann would be required to leave the premises. However, once Ann obtains a discharged or dismissal from chapter 7 or 13 bankruptcy, then the lender's attorney[13] will again continue with the foreclosure processing by resetting a sale (unless

---

12 In case of a non-judicial state, then there will be no court. So contact the lender directly with the suggestion of bankruptcy. The lender will be required to stop the foreclosure action at that point.

13 In case of non judicial state, then the sale will be reset by the trustee or whomever is assigned by the lender to move forward with its foreclosure.

the Chapter 13 plan, Ann brought the mortgage current, in which case, the foreclosure would be dismissed). The lender's attorney will inform the state court through a pleading that Ann is no longer under the protection of bankruptcy and to reset the sale.[14] The lender's attorney[15] would also lift the automatic stay once Ann has been discharged from bankruptcy court or the bankruptcy case has been dismissed. But it can take months, if not years, for the lender's attorney to get this far. As such, Ann can perhaps obtain a loan modification after she is discharged from a chapter 7 bankruptcy or other relief if she plans on keeping the home. If she files for chapter 13, then she will be paying on the home in her bankruptcy plan. In any event, chapter 7 and chapter 13 are awesome tools to delay foreclosure and buy the homeowner precious time.

How Does a Debtor Qualify for a Chapter 7 Bankruptcy?
In order to qualify for chapter 7 bankruptcy, a debtor must pass the means test. If someone can truly pay his debt, then he will not pass the means test. Under the old bankruptcy plan, prior to 2005, debtors would abuse the bankruptcy system. Prior to 2005, a debtor who could pay his credit card bills and other unsecured debt, would abuse the bankruptcy system by filing for chapter 7 or chapter 13 bankruptcy. Times changed. Today, a debtor has the burden of proving that he is insolvent (his monthly debt exceeds his monthly income). For the debtor to even consider filing for chapter 7, he must take and pass a means test.

How Does a Debtor Qualify for a Chapter 7 Bankruptcy?

The Means Test
A means test is calculated by deducting the debtor's monthly expenses from his monthly income. The debtor will not be able to file bankruptcy if the means test shows that the debtor income is too high or the debtor has a monthly

---

14 In a non-judicial procedure, the procedure might be a little different, but generally speaking, the lender will move forward once the borrower is no longer under bankruptcy protection.

15 In case of a non judicial state, then whoever is assigned by the lender to move forward with the foreclosure, will more than likely move the foreclosure forward.

positive cash flow after meeting his monthly obligation. So, basically, the debtor can only qualify for chapter 7 bankruptcy if the means test is satisfied.

Two Steps to the Means Test
You can pass the means test two ways:

Income More than the Median
For the very first step, ask yourself the following question: Is my current monthly income less than the median income of a household of my size in my state? If you answer yes to that question, then you are a candidate for chapter 7 bankruptcy. You have passed the means test and you can file for bankruptcy. You can get an average of your median income for your state or by checking my Firm's web page at www.stopforeclosurenowinflorida.com or by checking on http://www.foreclosuresurvivialguide.com/. You should also figure out what your household is. Are you the only person in the household? Do you have minors or other dependents that rely upon your income?

An Example of the Median Income and How to Calculate It.
Let us say Ann Brown lives in Broward county, Florida. Ann is a waitress and she makes $10,000 per year. Ann needs to file for Chapter 7. Ann would then have to find out if she passes the median test. She would do so by first calculating to see if her income is more than the median. So Ann checks out her median income by clicking on www. uscourts.gov. She looks for her state. Then she looks for her county. Then she looks for her job title. She notices that all other waitresses are making $15,000 and she only makes $10,000. At that point, Ann successfully passes the means test, because her income is less than the median. She has documentation to prove it. Her actual pay stub will be submitted to the bankruptcy court.

If your income does exceed the average median, do not worry. Just move on to the second way to pass the means test, and that is through using the means test calculator.

You will need a means test calculator. You can get one on line. My web page has one. Go to www.stopforeclosure-nowinflorda.com or http://www.foreclosuresurvivialguide.com/ and click on bankruptcy and click on 'means test.' The means test calculator is an easy way for you to calculate whether you will be eligible for chapter 7.

Using the Means Test Calculator
The very first step is for you to look up your zip code. This calculator is designed to use the proper income and expense that is standard in your state, your county and your region.

The second step is to calculate your state medium average. You should also fill out how many dependents are in your household and the size of your household. Then, from there, you should supply your income information. Then after that you should supply your expense information. The calculator will then let you know if you have passed the means test. You can save yourself time by writing down the information given from the means test. That way you can give that information to your attorney or you can use it to complete 22A of the bankruptcy paper work. The 22 A for bankruptcy can be found at www.uscourts.gov. Once you get there, click on forms and fees, and then scroll down and look for bankruptcy form. If you are unable to pass the means test, do not worry. You may still be a candidate for chapter 13 bankruptcy. See below on chapter 13.

Bankruptcy Forms for Chapter 7 or Chapter 13
You can obtain bankruptcy forms for chapter 7 or chapter 13 by clicking on www.uscourts.gov. Click on forms and click on chapter 7 or chapter 13. You can also visit your local United States district court and ask the clerk for the forms that you will need to file chapter 7 bankruptcy or chapter 13 bankruptcy.

When Will the Chapter 7 or Chapter 13 Be Dismissed or Discharged?
Chapter 7 and chapter 13 cases can be done away with in two ways. One way is for the court to discharge the case.

This would be a good thing. In a chapter 7 bankruptcy, this would mean that the federal judge has agreed to wipe out all your debt, and you will no longer be liable to pay it. And you will not owe any taxes on it, either. In a chapter 13, a discharge will happen after three years or five years (depends on how long your plan is for). This too would be a good thing because the federal judge is saying that once the monies are paid back according to the plan, you will no longer be obligated for the rest of the debt.

The next way is for a chapter 7 or chapter 13 bankruptcy case to be dropped is for the case to be dismissed. This would not be such a good thing because if the case gets dismissed, then you will not be able to wipe your debt out. The case gets dismissed usually because the debtor failed to attend the creditor's meeting, which is mandatory. The case gets dismissed because the debtor did not completely finish the application or the paper work that is required to file for chapter 7 or chapter 13. The case gets dismissed because the debtor did not completely follow the rules of the bankruptcy court. The case can get dismissed because the debtor does not qualify for either the chapter 7 or chapter 13 case that has been filed on behalf of the debtor. Regarding a foreclosure, once the case is dismissed, the lender's attorney will pick up back from where it left off.

Who Is the Trustee?
A bankruptcy trustee is appointed by the United States Court to administrate the debtor's bankruptcy estate. When the debtor files for bankruptcy under chapter 7, the debtor is saying to the court, "I want to liquidate whatever I have." When the debtor files for bankruptcy under chapter 13, the debtor is saying, "I want to create a payment plan to take care of my debt." Under the court system, we all have an estate. It does not matter whether we are rich or poor. As far as the court is concerned, we walk in the court house with an estate. It is who we are as people. It may be a joke for us to look at, but we are a walking estate under the United States Bankruptcy Court. This is my asset. This is

my debt. Good luck with my estate. I really have none.
The duty of the bankruptcy trustee is simple. Under chapter
7, the bankruptcy trustee is required by law to liquate all
the debtor's non-exempt property and distribute it to the
creditors according to the properties that the bankruptcy
code has established. Under chapter 13, the bankruptcy
trustee is required by law to redistribute the debtor's debt
by creating a payment plan that the debtor can live with
paying. Under a Chapter 7 or a Chapter 13, the trustee
also has a duty to consider whether the debtor has fraudu-
lently transferred assets. And if so, the trustee must recover
those fraudulent assets and recover them for the creditors
to get paid. If the trustee suspects that the bankruptcy system is being abused by the debtor, the trustee may bring a
motion to dismiss the case, or deny the debtor's discharge if
the trustee suspects that the debtor was involved with some
form of fraud, perjury or ineligibility.

Creditors Meeting and What to Expect
When it comes to filing bankruptcy (both chapter 7 and
chapter 13), debtors can expect to attend a mandatory
creditor's meeting. That meeting is called the 341 Creditor's
meeting. The meeting is usually held at least 15 days after
the debtor files for Chapter 7 bankruptcy or a few weeks
after the debtor files its repayment plan under chapter 13.
The meeting will be conducted by the United States Trustee.
The meeting invitation is extended to the debtor and the
debtors' creditors that have been listed on the bankruptcy
paper work. However, the creditors do not need to attend.
It is actually rare that a creditor attends, unless, of course,
the creditor would like to object to the debtor filing for
bankruptcy. During that meeting, the trustee will
swear in the debtor. It would be wise to attend this meeting
with your attorney, if you have retained one. If not, then
just be expected to answer a few short questions from the
trustee. The trustee will ask questions such as why the debtor
has filed for bankruptcy. The trustee will review the debtor's
application. The trustee will ask the debtor about the debt
that is involved. If a creditor is present, then the creditor

can object to the filing of bankruptcy. The trustee will ask the debtor if the debtor signed off on the bankruptcy petitioner. The trustee will also want to know if the debtor transferred any assets prior to filing for bankruptcy. It is presumed that this information is used by the trustee to recommend to the court and the judge whether the debtor's case is dischargeable and in a situation for chapter 13, whether the debtor can pay under the proposed bankruptcy plan. So when you go, be confident when you answer the questions because it may make the difference whether you are discharged from the debt or not or whether your chapter 13 plan gets approved.

How Will I Be Able to Save the Home Under a Chapter 7 and Chapter 13?

Let us say that you have obtained a full liquation of bankruptcy, because chapter 7 is full liquidation. If you want to save your home from foreclosure and you want to work things out with your lender, then you will have to fill out a portion of the bankruptcy sheet that allows for you to reaffirm the debt/redeem the property.

Under chapter 13, you will get to save the home because if you go through with bankruptcy, and the plan is approved, then you are catching up on your mortgage payments. You are paying back on the arrears over 36 and 60 months. So that is always a good sign.

Reaffirm the Debt/Redeem the Property

The trustee will always ask you what your intensions are for the home. At that point, you must tell the trustee that you want to keep the home. Make sure you do not leave the bankruptcy courthouse without filling out the reaffirmation of the debt. If you fail to do so, then the trustee will order for the home to be liquidated and at that point, *you will lose all your rights to fight for the home*. Reaffirmation means that the debtor and creditor again establish a relationship that they had before. As such, the debtor must pay and the creditor can keep suing to obtain the properties that are reaffirmed. So be sure if you want to keep the collateral that you will reaffirm; make sure you pay as you promised. If not, then the collateral (property including cars, house) can be taken from you. Visit www.uscourts.gov for obtaining the forms. If you have retained a bankruptcy attorney, then your bankruptcy attorney should know how to fill out the form.

Can Debtors Represent Themselves in a Chapter 7 Bankruptcy Case?
A long time ago, there was a saying that goes something like this: A woman who represents herself in court has a fool for a lawyer. Now you can take what you want from that. However, keep in mind that the average cost for filing for Chapter 7 is $1500.00 plus. Most bankruptcy attorneys will work with you on a payment plan. It may be well worth the fees, and it could save you a lot of headache. Particularly since the law has changed. Gone are the days when someone could just file bankruptcy on his own. Now it is well over 15 pages to file. It is electronic filing now. It may just be worth the fees to pay an attorney to file it for you.

Here Are a Few Questions to Ask Yourself When Considering Representing yourself:

1. Is your case very simple?
2. Will you be able to fill out forms completely?
3. Would it be wise to hire an attorney to save yourself time?

Since every bankruptcy case is unique, if you are really considering doing it yourself, it would be wise for you to review at minimum the forms involved. You should also be honest about the complexity of your case. The more complex it is the more likely it will be for you to have to hire an attorney. If you have a property that is in foreclosure, you perhaps will need to hire an attorney because at some point, you need to file for the suggestion of bankruptcy. Again, legal fees are now affordable with so many lawyers out there.

And with bankruptcy, most lawyers are willing to work with you on a payment plan.

What Is the Difference Between Chapter 7 and Chapter 13 Bankruptcy?

Chapter 7 and chapter 13 are very different types of bankruptcies. Chapter 7 is straight liquidation, which means the debtor does not get an opportunity to pay back the debt. But, of course, the debtor gets an opportunity to reaffirm the debt. Usually the debt that is being reaffirmed is often with a collateral, like a house or a car. Under chapter 13 bankruptcy, the debt does not have to be a house or collateral. A person can repay credit cards or other unsecured debt. Chapter 13 is often considered a restructuring of debt. The debtor must pay off the debt within three to five years. A good bankruptcy attorney will help a debtor save plenty from interest, as the debt gets paid down in three to five years. As such, most creditors look only to get paid back on the principle amount. It would be wise for a debtor to only pursue this avenue if the debtor has regular income, because if the debtor is unable to pay as the outline is scheduled, the trustee who supervises the case will recommend the court to dismiss it. And as such, the debtor will lose all.

How Can a Debtor Qualify for Chapter 13?

In order for a debtor to file for chapter 13, the debtor must have an income. The debtor must be able to document income. Unlike chapter 7—a person can be unemployed to file chapter 7. However, since chapter 13 is a repayment plan, you will have to prove to the court that you can repay the bankruptcy plan.

Who Can File for Chapter 13 Bankruptcy?

A debtor can only file for chapter 13 if the debtor has a regular income and the unsecured debt that is owed is less than $307,675. Examples of an unsecured debt would be credit cards and medical bills. Additionally, the secured debt such as a car and a home must be less than $922,975.

If the debtor is filing married and filing jointly, then both parties' unsecured debt must not exceed $307,675.00 and the secured debt must not exceed $922,975.00.

How Does Chapter 7 and Chapter 13 Bankruptcy Help a Homeowner Facing Foreclosure?

If you want to save your home, then consider chapter 7 or chapter 13. Both bankruptcies can help you save your home, because once you file for bankruptcy, then you receive an automatic stay.

Typical Foreclosure Scenario

Ann Brown lives in Broward County, Florida. Ann Brown has some creditor problems. She owes American Express $5000.00 on a credit card and ABC car dealership $10,000 on her 2002 Volvo s60. On top of that, she owes Bank of America $200,000 for her house that is now valued at $90,000.00. Ann Brown is facing a financial hardship. She received a pay cut because of the recession. Ann Brown feels very stressed out about her situation. She gets sick and tired of the creditors harassing her for money. She defaulted on her home and Bank of America is suing her under state court in a foreclosure action. So is American Express. Two days before Ann Brown's home went to the foreclosure auction block, Brown filed for bankruptcy protection under chapter 13. Ann Brown received her bankruptcy case number and her foreclosure attorney filed a suggestion of bankruptcy with the state court. Ann Brown saved her home from foreclosure. Because she obtained the automatic stay, Bank of America was required by law to cancel the sale date.

How Can a Chapter 13 Filing and Then Converting to a Chapter 7 Help a Homeowner Save her Home?

One reason you may need to get an attorney involved with filing your bankruptcy is because under certain situations, you can save your home by stripping the lien off your second lender. By doing so, you may be more than able to afford the home. A strip lien occurs when the Court takes off the lien off your home, or reduces the amount of secured lien attached to your home.

How Does it Work?

Ann Brown purchased a home in Florida for $375,000.00. Ann has a first mortgage with Ocean Bank for $50,000.00. Ann has a second mortgage with Pink Lady Bank for $200,000.00. During the real estate and economic boom, Ann made timely payments. In 2009, Ann fell behind on payments. On top of that, Ann's property value plummeted to $80,000.00. She immediately obtained an appraisal from her local property appraisal web page. Ann pays on her first mortgage, but falls behind on her second. Ann hires a bankruptcy attorney who advises Ann that she would be able to save her home if she strips lien the second lender. As such, the bankruptcy attorney takes Ann's paper work and he files a chapter 13 for Ann. At that point, the bankruptcy attorney strips the second lien, by obtaining a current value of Ann's home, (which was $80,000). As such, the second lender only obtained a secured interest for its loan by the U.S. Bankruptcy court for $30,000. I came up with that number by taking the value off the first from $50,000 and the equity left was $30,000 and so the second lender is secured up to $30,000. The $170,000 left over is now considered unsecured debt. The clever attorney then converted Ann's chapter 13 to a chapter 7. The $170,000 was discharged in the chapter 7 Bankruptcy. Ann saves her home because of the strip lien. Please also note that one does not have to convert the chapter 13 to a chapter 7. If you successfully strip your second lender off the loan, you can still finish up your chapter 13 plan and the balance will be dischargeable. A chapter 7 plan does not offer a strip lien.

Can I File Chapter 13 by Myself or Must I Hire an Attorney?

Homeowners do not have to hire attorneys to file for bankruptcy. In fact, a person never needs to hire an attorney for anything. Under the United States Constitution every citizen has the right to be heard. Every citizen has the right to file bankruptcy. However, it would be wise to hire an attorney because they know how to maneuver cases through the court system. They have been trained for years on doing that, while the average lay person has not. When it comes to bankruptcy, it is such a very cut-and-dried option. You can only file bankruptcy for a very short time. Here are reasons you should consider hiring a bankruptcy attorney:

1. *It will be done correctly*
   It is no surprise that the 2005 bankruptcy code has gotten tighter. Because it has gotten tighter, it is not uncommon for debtors to file the paper work and it ends up being wrong. In fact, Congress recently admitted that the bankruptcy code was written to let debtors hire attorneys. So if Congress' intent was to write the code that debtors hire attorneys, then you probably should not be tackling this paper work by yourself. Hire a bankruptcy attorney that is experienced. That way you can get the work done properly and you can get what you want–your home. If you end up doing the paper work incorrectly, then you will probably end up getting your case thrown out of court. Once the case gets thrown out of court, you will not receive the bankruptcy protection you need to save your home. Remember also that filing for bankruptcy is very stingy. You only get to do a Chapter 7 every seven years and a Chapter 13 perhaps every four years. So you do not want to be barred from filing Chapter 13 because you filed it wrong.

2. *The new bankruptcy law is not debtor friendly*
   The new bankruptcy code is not debtor friendly. A long time ago, a debtor could just file for bankruptcy and no one would question that debtor. All the debt would be wiped out. And the debtor did not even need an attorney to help him because the paper work was less than 15 pages, at most. However, after

2005, the creditors got tough. They recognize that people would just abuse the system because people who could pay their bills would rack up huge amount of debt and then get it wiped out. No one would question the debtor. As such, an abuse in the bankruptcy system occurred, which led to millions of dollars in loss to tax payers and to creditors. So the creditors came up with a brilliant idea. Why not just tighten up the bankruptcy code? So that the debtor has the burden of proving he really qualifies for bankruptcy. And to make things even tougher, the creditors came up with a plan. Let the debtors take certain courses and let the debtors go through many, many, many pages of paperwork. That should deter them. And guess what? It has. More debtors are finding a resistance to filing for bankruptcy. They have to take a pre-creditor course before filing. They must pass a means test to see if they qualify. Then they must fill out well over 15 pages of paperwork. They must also do a post creditor course, and the list goes on and on. They cannot file bankruptcy if they recently filed. If it is done incorrectly, things get kicked back and they can be barred from filing for bankruptcy. Because of this, it would be wise for a debtor to hire an attorney, because if the bankruptcy code is not debtor friendly, then the lawyer who is up on the law, can find loop holes that apply or advise the debtor on how to go about filing for bankruptcy. Bottom line, the bankruptcy lawyer's job is to make sure the debtor gets in the bankruptcy court and gets the debt wiped off. The lawyers who practice bankruptcy are very up on the law and always fight back against the creditor. They do what they can to get their clients in and out of bankruptcy court. A debtor without an attorney may not be so up on the law and may also not be as aggressive in going up against the creditor. After all, the debtor is not in the business of wiping debt on a daily basis. The attorney is.

3. You have a lot to lose—the roof over your head

The bankruptcy code is tough and the paper work is tight. If the bankruptcy is done wrong, then the case will get thrown out of court. If that happens and you are in foreclosure, you will not get the automatic stay, which means the creditor will be able to sell the home. If you really want to save your home, it may be worth the few dollars to invest in hiring an attorney. That way it will be done properly and you get to keep your home. The bankruptcy is really a one-shot deal. So take precautions and hire the experts so you get to keep the roof over your head.

Hint for Chapter 7 Dismissal or Discharge:

If you want to live rent free. Once your case has been discharged or dismissed, if you decide that you will just live rent free until the property is foreclosed, then do not call the lender. Let the lender find out on its own that your chapter 7 got dismissed or was discharged. Then let the lender do all the work needed to get the property back into a foreclosure status. Just work on monitoring the foreclosure. Clients have advised me that even after their chapter 7 gets dismissed or discharged, it is not uncommon for the lender to take well over seven months in initializing the foreclosure again. Once again, rent free living means you bank some bucks.

Chapter 6
How to Walk Away from Your Home with No Deficiency Judgment

Walking Away

If you decide to walk away from your home, you should consider doing two things. The first is to delay the foreclosure, so you can save enough money. Times are tough. The recession is taking a bite out of most American's savings. Since you already have the home, why not live there rent free so you can save money and then move on? Second, you should leave on your own terms, because if you just walk away, your lender may come after you if you signed a note that is restricted. Once the lender completes the foreclosure, if your state is a deficiency judgment state, then the lender will be able to seek the difference in what is owed. As such, you are better off negotiating to get that wave. You leave on your own terms, meaning, you are handing the keys to the bank with a few conditions. Those conditions are as follows:

1. The bank will not pursue you for the difference since the property value may drop.
2. The bank may repair your credit. (Some borrowers have gotten this done in a private settlement with the lender).
3. The short fall will not be treated as forgiveness of debt. Therefore, you owe IRS nothing.

What Is a Deficiency Judgment?

If the homeowner signed a note that says "with recourse" and the state the foreclosure is in recognizes Deficiency Judgments, like Florida, then the lender if it chooses can sue the homeowner for the short fall of the sale of the property. Imagine as a homeowner you have just lost your home to foreclosure. Then, to add insult to injury, the greedy lender decides to go after you for the short fall. That means you will be required to pay the bank thousands of dollars over years to come, for a home that you lost in foreclosure. If a bank obtains a Deficiency Judgment, then they can garnish the homeowner's wages. They can sell the homeowner's assets to satisfy the judgment. However, this can be avoided.

How to Avoid a Deficiency Judgment

John Brown lives in the state of Florida. John Brown purchased a home in Florida for $250,000.00. John Brown fell behind on his mortgage payment and his lender, Wall Bank, forecloses. Wall Bank obtained $100,000 for John's Brown home in the foreclosure. John Brown, who signed a note with recourse, obtained another lawsuit from Wall Bank. That lawsuit stated that Brown owed $150,000 to Wall Bank. Wall Bank obtained a judgment for $150,000.00 and Wall Bank garnished Brown's paycheck for $2000.00 per month (attempting to satisfy the judgment amount of $150,000.00). That is pretty scary stuff. Can this be avoided? Absolutely. Read below.

What State Do You Live In?

Even though a homeowner may sign a note that allows the lender to obtain a Deficiency Judgment, there are ways to avoid it. First of all, if you are in a state that does not allow for a Deficiency Judgment, then once the property is foreclosed, the bank cannot collect from you for the loss. Keep in mind as well, that just because the state recognizes a Deficiency Judgment doesn't mean your lender will move forward on it. The lender must pursue it (after the foreclosure is completed) and you must have signed a loan that is with recourse. A loan that is without recourse, even if the state recognizes a Deficiency Judgment, you will not obtain one because the loan that you sign does not allow the lender to go after you for the short fall once the property is foreclosed.

Here are a list of some of the states that recognizing a deficiency judgment as of October 2010.[16]

Alaska
Arizona
Arkansas
California
Colorado
District of Columbia (Washington DC)
Florida
Georgia
Hawaii
Idaho
Michigan
Minnesota
Mississippi
Missouri
Montana[17]
Nevada -
New Hampshire
North Carolina
Oregon
Rhode Island
South Dakota
Tennessee
Texas
Utah
Virginia

---

16 If you live in a state that is not included on the above reference list, it would be wise to check your state Statute, just to make sure your state does not recognize a deficiency judgment. Due to brevity, at times reference checks for researching this book, are just outline and does not completely narrow or focus on one state. So do additional research to collaborate with this information.

17 In the state of Montana, a Deficiency Judgment will only be obtained if the lender pursues the foreclosure as a non-judicial foreclosure.

Washington
West Virginia
Wyoming

File for Chapter 7 or Chapter 13 Bankruptcy
If you are in a state that recognizes Deficiency Judgment and you signed a note that allows for the lender to collect, then you can avoid one by filing for chapter 7 bankruptcy or chapter 13 bankruptcy. For more information see chapter 5, which details chapter 7 and chapter 13 bankruptcy.

Hire a Competent Attorney
If you have signed a note that allows a Deficiency Judgment, then you may want to contact a real estate attorney or a lawyer that specializes in foreclosure. Hiring a competent lawyer who can negotiate with the lender to waive the judgment may save you thousands of dollars or save you from a Deficiency Judgment. This may be the one time you may want to invest in hiring an attorney who has the skills to get the lender to waive the Deficiency Judgment.

Become Judgment Proof
You can always avoid a Deficiency Judgment if you are insolvent. Insolvent means that your liability exceeds your income and assets. If you are the head of the household, and a lender obtained a judgment against you, you can always raise that as a defense. If you have no assets and your income is below a certain level, then even if the lender obtains a judgment, they will not be able to collect on it. But check your state and federal guidelines to see if you fall under the exception. There is a possibility for you to have assets that the lender is not entitled to collect. Those assets must be recognized as an exemption under your State Law or some Federal Statute.

If also the assets you have are exempted under state or federal guidelines, then the lender will not be able to collect on it. Almost everyone's 401 k and IRA retirement plans are exempted from creditors. But again, it is state specific.

Recently, I came across a self-employed client who was being sued by his lender and he needed help defending against a garnishment. I reside in the State of Florida and practice law there. The self-employed borrower had a sep IRA and a self-employed 401k. It turned out after checking the law in detail in Florida, the self-employed 401k would be game for the creditor. So that self-employed borrower may have to turn the self-employed 401k asset over to the creditor. So again, it would be wise to check your state law and check the federal guidelines for exemption. That way, your assets will be well protected from your lender who forecloses and seeks to collect on its judgment. Other exempted property that state and federal law may include is life insurance proceeds and certain cars and certain income. For a list of those exemptions, you should consult an attorney who specializes in bankruptcy, asset protection or consumer law. Do not leave anything to chance and do not assume that you will be okay.

Negotiate with the Lender to Release You from the Deficiency Judgment
Foreclosure can be a scary thing and the homeowner will be facing a great loss. The homeowner loses the home, money and credit. But there are ways to reduce the loss. For example, it would be wise for the homeowner to avoid the Deficiency Judgment altogether. That way, once the foreclosure is complete, the homeowner can walk away and start over without the headache or the worries of whether the lender will garnish pay checks and other assets. So the best way to avoid the Deficiency Judgment would be to try during the foreclosure to negotiate with the lender to release you from it. Two ways to do this may be a short sale and Deed in Lieu of foreclosure. For more information on short sale and Deed in Lieu, please see chapters 7 and 8, respectively.

DO SOMETHING!!!!!!
Again, I cannot emphasis the importance to homeowners of doing something. It would be better to over-prepare

than under-prepare. If you do nothing and then the lender gets a Deficiency Judgment and it decides to sue you, then your pay checks will be garnished. Imagine waking up one morning to find that you check your bank account and your account is overdrawn. Not because you did not make a deposit but because your lender who foreclosed on your home that happened to have a Deficiency Judgment on it, that was awarded to the lender while you were in fore-closure and your state recognized it. How sad that would be when it could have been avoided. Let us say that you somehow got it cleared up.   You hire an attorney who ended up negotiating on your behalf with the lender or you file for bankruptcy. I know one thing for sure. Once the money is gone, you won't be getting it back. You may be able to protect against future garnishment, but you will have to live with the consequences on the old garnishment. It will be a nightmare. And I am talking from experience. I get a lot of calls with crying borrowers who have gone temporarily insane because the lender who forecloses on their home obtained a Deficiency Judgment and now their bank accounts are being seized to pay for the judgment. Personally, I think it adds salt to the wound. In foreclosure, you already have to give the lender your home. Why give them your paycheck?

Chapter 7
Doing a Short Sale to Stall Foreclosure or Walking Away with Little Liability

What Is a Short Sale?

When a homeowner is facing foreclosure, the homeowner must try to reduce his liability and tax consequences. It is bad enough that the homeowner is losing the home. But if the homeowner sits down and does nothing, the lender can complete a foreclosure and then seek to sue the homeowner later for the short fall of the mortgage. So the homeowner should understand perhaps negotiating terms with the lender in giving back the property would help to reduce the borrower's liability. Once such way a borrower can reduce liability is by obtaining a short sale. A short sale occurs when the borrower is upside down on his mortgage payment. That happens when the house the borrower is trying to sell or is being foreclosed on has no equity, and the value of the home is less than what is owed on the mortgage. As such, the borrower needs to get the lender to agree to accept a lessor amount and the borrower needs the lender to forgive the debt.

How to Obtain a Short Sale

In order to obtain a short sale, the borrower must hire a competent real estate attorney, a competent accountant and a competent realtor.

Real Estate Attorney

It would be wise to hire a real estate attorney, because in certain jurisdictions, the lender can still obtain a Deficiency Judgment against the short fall. As such, the lender may be able to sue the borrower at a later time for the short fall, and if a judgment is successfully obtained by the lender, then the borrower could be paying the lender back for years on the short fall. A real estate attorney will be able to help negotiate the release of the Deficiency Judgment or the real estate attorney will at minimum be able to tell you whether your jurisdiction or loan falls under the Deficiency Judgment and they will advise you on how to avoid it. A real estate attorney will also be able to help negotiate the contract with the bank, and they may be able to help negotiate for the bank to release you from all future judgments.

Competent Accountant

Let us say John Brown, the borrower, faces foreclosure. He purchased the property for $200,000.00 and his loan amount is $160,000.00. He only owes one mortgage on the property. However, the value of the property is around $100,000.00. John Brown decides that he would like to just walk away from the home with very little consequences from the lender. Therefore, John Brown decides to obtain a short sale. During the short sale, Brown gets a buyer to pay $100,000.00 for the home. Brown brings this short sale to the bank and the bank agrees to accept $100,000.00. Then, as is customary with most short sales, the bank releases the lien against the property for only $100,000.00, and the $60,000.00 the bank decides to forgive the debt releases Brown and 1099's him for $60,000.00. This is where a competent accountant comes in. When a short sale goes through and the bank agrees to take less, the bank will generally issue a forgiveness of debt to the borrower. As such, the borrower will be receiving a 1099 and is subject to owing the IRS money. The IRS treats the forgiveness of debt as income. How can John Brown or any troubled borrower in this predicament avoid paying the IRS income? It would be wise to hire a competent attorney before you even consider the short sale. Under the Mortgage Forgiveness Debt Relief Act of 2007, the IRS will consider the debt forgiveness income. However, since every borrower's financial dilemma is unique, an accountant will help determine if you have enough tax losses to offset the 1099 income, which means you would owe IRS nothing. Additionally, there are exceptions to the Mortgage Forgiveness Debt Relief Act of 2007, (HR 3648). If the short sale was obtained against the borrower's primary residence, then the IRS will not treat the 1099 as income, which means the borrower will owe the IRS nothing. But if the borrower cashes out on the primary residence or refinances it, then that can pose as income, unless the cash out was used to fix the primary property. Again, this book is limited to this information and the best way to make sure you owe the IRS nothing is to seek the advice of a competent accountant before you even sign off on the short sale. If a short sale leaves you with income tax consequences, then you are probably better off filing for bankruptcy, which will discharge you of liability. So look around at your options before gunning away at getting out of your foreclosure dilemma. The goal should be to walk away with very little tax consequences and judgments from your bank. It is bad enough that you are losing the home.

Hire a Realtor Who Has Experience in Short Sales

A short sale is a very long and tedious process. It is not uncommon for the borrower to go for months without obtaining a short sale. The average short sale as of October 2009 takes as long as six months to close. Many short sales do not go through for a few reasons:

1. The red tape in contacting the lender is too tedious and most people just give up. It is not uncommon for borrowers to just get the run-around from the lender's side.
2. The realtor who is involved lacks the experience in conducting a short sale.
3. The decision maker for the lender has not been identified or has not been contacted.

Let us look carefully at the realtor involved. If you really want to obtain a short sale, it would be best for you to hire a realtor who has experience in short sales. As you know, practice makes perfect. If a realtor has worked on many short sales and successfully obtains them, then that is the realtor you want to use. Most realtors do not even know what a short sale is, let alone get you one. Other realtors refused to work on short sales, because they lack the patience and diligence to work on obtaining the banks' decision maker. Since obtaining a short sale may be the difference in you not paying the bank, then do your homework. Start by calling up friends or families who are in the same boat as you. Call up the realtors you know. Ask them about their expertise in short sales. Find out if they have worked with your lender. Find out how many short sales they have closed. Find out everything and don't be afraid to ask them for references. And don't be afraid to contact those references. This little homework you are doing in hiring a short sale expert may be the difference in your walking away from your foreclosure with very little liability. So now is not the time to panic about your situation. You can get the results you need. You just have to do a little leg work.

What Are the Documents Needed to Obtain a Short Sale?

In order to obtain a short sale, the lender will require certain documentations from you:

1. *Letter of authorization*

You will need to sign a letter of authorization if you have retained the service of a realtor or an attorney. The letter of authorization just allows the lender to speak with the realtor or attorney about your property (see the appendix for a sample authorization letter).

2. *Preliminary net sheet*

The lender loves to obtain the paperwork, which reflects the numbers. The primary net sheet shows to the lender what the loss will be, once the purchase price, the taxes, and realtor fees are paid.

3. Hardship letter

The lender wants to know why you are not able to keep the home. Of course the only rational reason is that you suffered some form of hardship (see the appendix for sample hardship letter).

4. Proof of income and assets

In order to obtain a short sale, you better let the bank know you are dirt poor. Dirt poor means your debt exceeds your income and you have no assets. Think about it. The bank will be releasing you from all liability. Why on earth would it release someone who has assets? That will make no sense for the bank who is a profitable organization and the sole purpose of loaning money is to make a profit. Exempted assets may not be considered a factor, like 401ks and retirement. However, Banks may request that borrowers pull money out of retirement to help pay for the short fall. It would be very foolish for a borrower to do so. Don't let the bank intimidate you on taking your hard-earned cash. Say no and don't do the short sale if you are required to sell off your 401k. If you put up a fight, the bank will still approve it. But you have to convince the bank that you have no assets.

5. Copies of your most recent bank statements

The lender does not want to release you from a mortgage if you have the ability to pay. As such, the lender would like to see your recent bank statements, to see if you are doing a strategic foreclosure. Remember there are some people who just do not want the home because the value is not there.

6. Comparative Market Analysis

The comparative market analysis provides the lender with the value of your home. It is done by a licensed appraisal or a licensed realtor. The realtor or appraisal will look up your property and based upon that, it will pull around four homes that are similar to yours that were sold within six months from the date you signed the listing agreement. The bank will then adjust up or down the value of your home depending on whether your home is superior or inferior. For instance, if a home sold six months ago like yours without a pool and yours has a pool, then the bank will add around $10,000 more to your home because of the pool. If a home sold six months ago that is five bedrooms and yours is four bedrooms, then the bank will take around $15,000 off your value because your home has less room.

7. *Purchase Agreement and Listing Agreement*

Since most people who are doing a short sale engaged a licensed realtor, the realtor will have you sign a listing agreement. A listing agreement is signed by the broker and the buyer. It lists the conditions of selling the home. It lists the purchase price and the commission to be paid. It might also list the MLS (multiple listing service) number. The lender needs this so that it can see if the listing agreement is an arms-length transaction, which means the buyer is not your family member.

The purchase agreement will be done once the borrower obtained a buyer. The lender needs this as well. It will list the purchase price and the date of the closing and the conditions that the seller will meet prior to closing.

Living Rent Free While You Obtain the Short Sale

Keep in mind, while you are negotiating your short sale, if you are in foreclosure, then you will not have to pay your property taxes, your mortgage or your insurance. Since a short sale may take as long as six months to go through, you can stay in the foreclosure home and basically live rent free for those six months. Of course, you will have to pay your utility bills. While living rent free, you can save money to rent a home, or you can save money which would help you make up for some of the bad loss from the mortgage. To maximize your ability to live rent free, once a foreclosure complaint has been filed against you, hire an attorney who can file an answer. That way, you can always let the court know you are negotiating with a short sale and not to auction the property off as you are working something out with the lender. If you fail to preserve your legal defenses, then the discretion of accepting a short sale lies with the lender and if the lender refuses to accept a short sale, you will lose the property in foreclosure.   But again, it doesn't matter. Foreclosures are so backed up these days that if you just stay in the property, you can save some money, because you will not have a mortgage to pay.[18]

---

18 You can still live rent-free in a non-judicial state. The lenders will generally hold off on foreclosure if it is entertaining a sweet short sale deal.

Chapter 8
Obtaining a Deed in
Lieu of Foreclosure

What Is a Deed in Lieu of Foreclosure?
One sure way to walk away from your foreclosure without owing the IRS or the lender anything is getting a Deed in Lieu. This is a very secret weapon that the lender does not want you to know about because (1) it puts the property back in the lender's hands and the lender doesn't have to foreclosure on the home and (2) you walk away with no judgment. And that means less money for the lender. Follow this book and the instructions in it and if you are in foreclosure, consider the Deed in Lieu. Here are some of the advantages of a Deed in Lieu:

1. *It is less of a hassle and less of a stress than a foreclosure.*
   A foreclosure can be a very stressful thing. Imagine you wake one morning to a loud knock on your door. A sheriff is at the door with foreclosure papers. It gives you 20 days to respond and from there on the complaint list wants everything from you. This paper, the complaint generally gives homeowners anxiety because they are not sure how long they will be in the property and don't forget, there might be a count two that allows the bank to obtain a Deficiency Judgment, which means even when the foreclosure is over, the homeowner will be paying the banks for years. That makes no sense. On the other hand, a Deed in Lieu is simple. Once the

lender accepts the Deed in Lieu proposal, then all the homeowner needs to do is sign away the deed. And the lender releases the homeowner from the judgment and the liability. Why not do that?

2. *You get released from liability, which means no judgment.* If the lender accepts the Deed in Lieu, one require- ment of the Deed in Lieu is that the agreement means the lender must release the homeowner from the Deficiency Judgment. If the homeowner is released from the Deficiency Judgment, then the lender will not be able to collect any money from the loss of the prop- erty when the lender goes to sell it.

How Does a Deed in Lieu Work?

There will be two documents required to be signed when you go to obtain a Deed in Lieu of foreclosure. Those docu- ments are an **agreement in lieu of foreclosure** and a **war- ranty deed**, **quit claim deed** or a **grant deed**. An agree- ment in lieu of foreclosure outlines the terms and conditions of the Deed in Lieu. It must be signed by the lender and borrower in order to be effective. The deed will give legal ownership to the property. It will be signed by the bor- rower. The borrower's note becomes paid and the lender will mark it paid. The lender then issues to the borrower a form that states the debt has been cancelled. The lender will also issue another form which waives the lender's right to a Deficiency Judgment. Usually an escrow company will execute the agreement for Deed in Lieu. The lender will send to the escrow company the borrower's note as paid. The escrow company will be responsible for recording the deed. The deed transfers legal ownership of the mort- gaged property. Once transferred, the escrow company sends the borrower the note and the borrower is released from the mortgage payment and from liability.

A deed in lieu is usually prepared by the lender or the hom- eowner's attorney and it will be filed in the public records of where the property is located. Bear in mind that a Deed in Lieu is a harder hit on the credit than a foreclosure. But also keep in mind that you can always restore your credit. Moreover, you are avoiding stress from the foreclosure and a Deficiency Judgment, which saves you thousands of dollars.

How Do You Obtain a Deed in Lieu?

There are some restrictions in obtaining a Deed in Lieu. For instance, you must only have one mortgage attached to the property. Therefore, homeowners who are facing foreclosure and have a first and a second mortgage will not be able to obtain a Deed in Lieu. The rule is simple: Only one mortgage can be attached to the property.

Here is other information that will be needed in order to obtain the Deed in Lieu:

1. Updated financial information is needed for all parties on the loan.
2. Interior appraisal.
3. Title reports, to ensure that the property is free and clear of any liens or encumbrances.
4. Premises must be vacated once homeowner signs the deed over to lender.
5. Completed Deed in Lieu documents.
6. Bank statements.
7. Listing agreement from the seller's realtors, showing a good-faith attempt to sell the home.
8. Tax returns.
9. Social Security card and driver's license.

Keep in mind that the above are just a few of the documents and requirements that may be needed. Lenders vary. But, over the years of completing the Deed in Lieu, it appears that lenders generally request the information above.

Restrictions to the Deed in Lieu

Now that you know that a Deed in Lieu is a very powerful tool in helping to solve your foreclosure crisis, keep in mind that you may not always obtain one.

The following reasons are why you may not obtain the Deed in Lieu:

1. You will not obtain a Deed in Lieu if there are any tax liens, second lien holders or a homeowners' association lien. As such, you must be current on your property taxes and your homeowner association fee. The lender will not approve a Deed in Lieu with any encumbrances.
2. You must prove to the lender that you have attempted to sell the property and you were not able to. The lender will look at the listing agreement for such proof.

But again, check with your lender, as each lender requirement may vary and as the foreclosure crisis become increasing, perhaps lenders will slack their rules to acquire property through deed in lieu.

Are There Tax Consequences to a deed in Lieu?
When it comes to a Deed in Lieu of foreclosure, you will not have a Deficiency Judgment as you can always get an attorney to have the lender release you. However, the lender will send you a 1099 and that 1099 is reported to the IRS as income. With all these foreclosure issues, it would be wise to consult or hire an attorney and/or an accountant, as there are always exceptions to the rule. Remember, every homeowner's issue is unique. Let us now dive into ways to avoid the tax consequences that are associated with a Deed in Lieu. Here are some examples for you to follow:

Let us say that Mary Jane purchased a property at $500,000 in 2005. She refinanced it in 2007 for $700,000. Mary is now under foreclosure in 2009, the property in foreclosure is her primary residence and it is only worth $300,000. It's terrible that Mary is losing her credit and her investment. So let us see how Mary can get away with no tax consequences from the IRS. Let us also see how Mary can get away from paying the bank for years. Let us say that Mary does not want to go through with foreclosure. She just wants to give the property back to the lender with little or no liability. This recession is a mess and Mary just wants to give the property back and the bank actually accepts Mary's proposal and it gives her the Deed in Lieu with a 1099. The 1099 gets reported to the IRS. Now Mary is going to figure out how to get out of the 1099. So she will first do some research and that research is also available to you. Okay, so here is the situation for Mary. Let us say Mary got the Deed in Lieu of foreclosure. She perhaps gets a 1099. But Mary does not have to worry because the tax law gives a few exemptions.

Let us say that the day Mary gave the property to the bank, in a Deed in Lieu of foreclosure, Mary was insolvent. Insolvent means Mary's debt exceeds her assets. So, therefore, if the bank gave Mary a 1099 that day, when she was insolvent, then Mary is not liable for taxes because she is insolvent.

Let us say another day that Mary is not insolvent, but she is eligible for chapter 7 bankruptcy. Then Mary gets to walk away from paying the IRS because, according to the law, even if Mary is not insolvent, the fact that she is a candidate for bankruptcy means she gets to wipe out the 1099 and she owes no taxes to the IRS. Wow. Mary is very happy now. All Mary has to do is file for chapter 7 bankruptcy, and she would be discharged from the 1099.

Let us say that she is neither insolvent nor a candidate for bankruptcy. That is not a problem. Recent law is changing and it says that Mary can exclude her 1099, which means she does not pay the IRS a thing even if she is solvent. Therefore, recent 1099s, recent bankruptcies, and recent foreclosures may fall under some special circumstances.

If I were Mary, I would first hire a foreclosure attorney and a CPA who could show me those loopholes. Therefore Mary will owe nothing to the IRS. How lovely life would be. Hire the experts. It makes a difference whether Mary swims or whether Mary drowns. Self is very important. So look out for yourself and hire the experts.

What to Expect from a Deed in Lieu

The following situation is just a scenario, but it will help you feel comfortable in just what to expect with the Deed in Lieu. Mary Jones is having financial difficulties. She is now three months behind on her mortgage payments. Foreclosure is around the corner. Mary knows that she signed a note and that if a foreclosure is completed, then the bank can obtain a Deficiency Judgment and the bank may go after Mary for thousands of dollars for the loss of the home. So Mary calls her local realtor and she lists the property for sale, at a lower price, hoping to obtain a short sale, because she is selling the property for less than what is it worth. After five months, Mary has gotten no bites on her property. There is just no buyer. The property is already in foreclosure and Mary decides that she would rather give the bank the property back and have it releases her from the judgment. She wants to avoid foreclosure. Mary calls the lender. She speaks to someone in the loss mitigation department. Mary then explains to her lender's loss mitigation staff that she wants out. The lender then mails Mary a package. In that package, the lender outlines to Mary what is required to obtain a Deed in Lieu. It has the instructions and the documents that the lender would want from Mary.

Mary then gathers all the documents and Federal expressed them to the lender. The lender then receives them and, within a few more days, Mary receives a call from the lender's appraiser. The appraiser wants to appraise the property. This includes doing an interior check on the value of the house. Mary agrees and she sets a time and date for the appraiser to have access to the property, including the inside of the home. The appraisal then gets done.

Mary then receives another call from the lender. The lender Federal expressed to Mary the Deed in Lieu document, that the lender's attorney prepared. Mary then signs off on the Deed in Lieu. At that moment, the property is transferred to the lender. And Mary leaves the home and she Federal expressed the house key(s) to the lender. The lender now owns the property and Mary walks away. Mary then receives a 1099 from the lender. Mary has completed her Deed in Lieu.

Chapter 9
Stalling Foreclosure While You Live Rent Free

Keep in mind that this chapter has to do with judicial states. So this chapter will only be able to help homeowners who are in a judicial foreclosure state where the lender is suing the homeowner in court. See chapter one for a recap of the judicial states, but still read below to pick up some ideas that must be tailored to fit a non-judicial state.[19]

Many homeowners ask why on earth someone would want to stall the foreclosure process. Well, here is the main reason:

Live Rent Free
If you are underwater with your property, you may feel cheated by the lender. You may have run out of money trying to pay for the darned property. You may also come to terms with the fact that you will never be able to make your money back. So, the best thing to do would be to get some of your money back if you can. Let me be blunt. Sometimes buying real estate is just a bad deal. It is a bad deal because sometimes homes are not able to be liquidated and I don't need to tell you too much. You are already seeing the bad deals real estate can make. People run out of money by paying for them. People not only run out of money

---

19 Non-Judicial States can still delay foreclosure through, short sales, deed in lieu, bankruptcy or they can take advantage on the back log every lender faces today. Most lenders are just not prepared to handle the hurdle of millions of foreclosure homes that will flood the real estate market.

by paying for them, but sometimes you buy a property and you do not always get your money back. So a way most troubled borrowers are making up for some of their losses is just to live in their homes rent free.

Rent, Free: How Did that Come About?

Let's take a state like Florida. As of 2010, if a bank forecloses on you, it will take it at least one year to get it through the court system. Since it takes that long to go through the court system, the homeowner can wait for the sheriff to knock on the door. As such, the homeowner can live rent free until that day comes.

Example of Rent Free Living

Pam James purchased a home and her mortgage payments are $2000.00 per month. Pam is underwater (which means she owes more than it's currently worth on the market) with the house, so she chooses to no longer make a payment. Pam lives in Florida, which is a judicial foreclosure state, and so Pam's bank must go through the court system to foreclose on Pam. Since the foreclosure will take approximately 12 months, Pam will be able to save around $24,000.00, since she is living rent free. If it takes another 12 months, that would be a total of $48,000.00 that Pam pockets once the foreclosure is completed. Since home values have dropped substantially, Pam can purchase another home with the $48,000.00 as a down payment. Pam can also use a cosigner since her credit would be ruined and it may take years to repair. Pam may also opt to pay a higher interest rate, since she has a good amount for a down payment. The bottom line is, because the home is now in foreclosure, Pam has an option which allows her to save.

What You Can Do with the Money from Living Rent Free

Keep in mind that a troubled borrower lives rent free, but her credit rating will be shot. It may take years to repair it. However, I have heard of people using credit repair companies to restore their credit rating. Here are some options if the troubled borrower decides to live rent free:

1. *Start a New Business*

American is founded upon the ideal of capitalism. It may sound crazy, but in America, people are rewarded for starting up businesses. Unfortunately, there is a tremendous amount of risk that goes into starting a business. But the good side is if the business works, then the person can take the company to endless grounds. However, in order to even contemplate starting a business, you need to have the capital. And if you are not born into a very affluent family, you will have to find a way to borrow it, talk people into lending you the money or save for it. Imagine if you are in foreclosure and you hate your job. You always dream about having your own business, but you did not have the balls to do it. Or you did not want to take the risk. Or you just did not have the money to start out. Well, if you are thinking in terms of opportunity, perhaps being in foreclosure is not such a bad thing at all. Yes, I understand the bank ruined your credit and sold you a really bad loan. But think of the positive. You are not paying a mortgage while you are in foreclosure. Therefore, you can always use the mortgage money to finally start your dream business. All it takes is capital. So let us say your mortgage is $1000 per month, and you foreclosure is delayed for 12 months. That would be $12,000.00 to start a business. More than ever, a business is cheap to start today, thanks to the internet. You can build a web page for less than $500.00 and you can run a business out of your house, if you have the proper documentation from the State, town, or the City to do so. Additionally, it has been proven that most successful businesses get their start from the house. That means many entrepreneur started off working from their home. They had so much confidence in

themselves, they did not need a big office to vali-
date them. They did not need the general public to
size them up based upon where their head office is.
So, if you have a burning desire to run a business and
you can keep the costs really low, and now that you
are in foreclosure, you can find the costs, then go for
it. You only get one shot at this life. Live it. Do what
you think will make you happy.

2. *Savings*

Most people do not recognize this, but if you are living in a property rent free, then you can save money,
since the largest expense one faces is housing. So
let us say Jill Smith is facing foreclosure. She hires a
foreclosure attorney who files the proper paperwork
with the court, causing a long delay. The attorney
informed Jill Smith that there will not be a sale on her
home for at least two years. Ms. Smith keeps her job
and she makes $3000 per month. Usually Ms. Smith
pays a mortgage of $1500 per month. Because
she does not have a mortgage payment, Ms. Smith
saves $1500 per month. In 10 months, Ms. Smith has
$15000.00. In 20 months, Ms. Smith has $30,000.00
saved. Now, I know Ms. Smith no longer has credit.
But I think with $30,000 saved, she can do plenty. If she
finds a cosigner, then she can get another home in no
time. If she follows the Fannie Mae guidelines, even
with really bad credit, with the amount she is putting
down, she can get into another house. Keep in mind
that house prices are very low. Therefore, Ms. Smith
will be able to get another home. In Florida, there are
plenty of townhomes selling for in the Miami and Fort
Lauderdale area for $100,000.00. When the market
was very high, these homes were selling for $280,000
with no money down. Now at $100,000, all you need
is 20% down, and that brings you to $20,000.00. The
payments will be so much more affordable. It would
be a no brainer to just stay in foreclosure just to
save money. Make the best use of a bad situation.

Then again, who told you that foreclosure was a bad situation? Perhaps it was the greedy bank, who did not want you to cash out on your misfortune.

3. *Pay Off other Debt*

In America, the financial system is based upon credit. At times, many consumers are just strapped with credit and very little cash to meet their monthly obligations. It appears that some troubled borrowers in foreclosure are losing their home, because they over-borrowed and they cannot meet their monthly obligations. But things do not have to be that gloomy. Imagine if you were living rent free and you had very high credit card and car payments. Let us take James Brown. James is a middle class American. He makes around $3000 per month. He has a Mercedes Benz, for which he pays $500.00 per month. His car insurance is $200.00 per month.   He also has five credit cards, which are all maxed out, and he pays around $700.00 per month on the minimum payment. His daughter attends private school for $500.00 per month and his mortgage is $1500 per month. This leaves James in the negative every month of $200.00. This does not even include light, water, and groceries. However, James just juggles his bills and he has used his credit cards to help finance his lifestyle. His lifestyle is not even that lavish. Most of the credit card debt was used to pay for food, medical bills and gas. At some point, by paying for food, medical bills and gas, the credit cards just maxed out over time. It took James over five years to max them out. James has had enough of all these bills and he is hoping for a miracle. But, to add insult to injury, his mortgage is about to adjust from 6% to 12%. That means his mortgage payment will double. The mortgage company had assured him to take the mortgage because the house would double in price.   At the time James bought his house, prices in Florida were appreciating around 25% per month. So the mortgage company told him he would be rich and he would be stupid not to take the adjustable mortgage. So he did as the mortgage company told him.

Unfortunately, the bottom of the barrel in the housing market dropped out, causing James to lose his shirt and his life savings in the real estate market. The value of James' house plummeted. To make matters worse, the mortgage payments double and the mortgage company places James into foreclosure. While that happened, James hired a foreclosure attorney who kept defending the home and advised James he had three years in the property to live rent free. While James lived in the home, he used the mortgage money to pay off his credit card debt. Once that was done, he contacted his attorney and requested loan modification documentation. He then contacted the bank and obtained a loan modification. James provided the proper documentation and the lender reduced his interest rate. At that point, James was able to pay for the mortgage and he was able to do so with ease, because he did not have any debt at all, just the home. What just happened here? The borrower James, created his own stimulus package, by paying off debt, while he stalled the foreclosure.

4. *Spend More Time with Family*
Let us face it. In America, we work a lot of hours. Our time is very important to us in this country. We get exactly 30 minutes to one hour of lunch time. We have to show up to work on time. We work around eight to nine hours per day and then we have two days to see our spouse and children. We then get about one week of vacation per year, with perhaps the maximum of two weeks of vacation time. If we are lucky, maybe we can coordinate the vacation time with our spouse and we can get good time off. I know couples that work for years and they are unable to take vacations together because their jobs

will not grant the time that is needed. So what am I saying here? So imagine you are in foreclosure and you were working two jobs before that. Now that you do not have a mortgage payment, maybe you can take it easy and relax. I mean, you were probably working because you had to meet your monthly obligation of the loan and other expenses. If you do not have to meet the house expense, then you can just relax and then you can just start spending more time with your family.

Wouldn't it be nice to see your children or spouse a few extra hours or a few extra days? Life is not always about material things. I can tell you as an attorney, I have the privilege and pleasure of working with very diverse people. I can tell you I have seen people who are facing foreclosure make the best of it. They spend time with their family. They cut down on working two jobs, so they can spend time with their families, or one spouse gives up her job, in order to care for the young children and home. Then they recognize, once they are out of foreclosure, that they will perhaps be better off downsizing because the sacrifice of staying home with a child is more than worth it.

It appears that children too are happy when they see their father and mother. Life and time are not always measured in dollars and cents. So if you are in foreclosure, start thinking about what is important to you and start prioritizing. Use this opportunity to restructure your life and your goals.

You could also choose to use the money to start a new business, or pay off other debt that has been holding you back. You could also use the money to pay off your car payment or to buy health insurance coverage. The fact that you went into foreclosure has provided you with many options.

5.   Save the Home

Let's face it.   Most people bought their homes because they love them. They love the kitchen. They love the garage. They love the stove. They love the fireplace. For some reason, the person just loves the home. And because people love their home, they will be emotionally attached to it. They look around and they love the colors of the room they painted and it reminds them of them. And for that reason, people would do anything to save their home, because they love it. And that is why they bought it to begin with. So it does not matter to some people that they have lost $100,000 in value on their house. As far as there are concerned, who cares? They love the darned place and they want to pay off for it so they can leave it for their children. So what point am I trying to make? When a person loves the home, he is going to save it, because he is emotionally attached to it. So if you love your home, and you are in foreclosure, shouldn't you save it?   Absolutely you should, and there are ways to do so. Below is a list of ways to save your home from foreclosure.

a. **Correct why you are in foreclosure**- if you are in foreclosure due to a loss of job, then get another job that pays enough for you to afford the home.
b. **Consider a loan modification**- if you have a loan that is about to adjust higher and you will not be able to pay for the mortgage amount, request loan modification information from your lender.
c. **Use the Opportunity to Live Rent Free to Pay Off Debt**

Okay, at times strategic foreclosure is a good thing. I have a client that is in foreclosure and she can't afford her home. She makes good income, but unfortunately she has a lot of debt. She owes American Express $5000.00 and Discover $5000.00 and she has a Mercedes Benz that she owes $30,000.00 on. Hey, it's South Florida. People have to look good here. Anyway, because of these high debts, she cannot afford her house payment. So my firm advised her that while she is in foreclosure, she should use that mortgage money to pay off other debt. That way, when it is time to save the home, she will have little or no debt and she for sure will be able to qualify for the mortgage payment. And it worked. After 10 months of being in foreclosure, my client submitted her loan modification package and she was approved because her debt to income ratio was no longer high. In fact, for the first time in her life, she had savings. The bank was excited and immediately approved her because her debt to income ratio finally made sense. Keep in mind that during a loan modification, the lender does not care about credit score. So under this scenario, credit score does not matter, because the client already owned the home. What the lender cared about was the client's ability to pay. The only way the client could show that she could pay was to have her debt to income ratio intact. That is 31% of her gross income. End of story, the client saved the home, by using the time she had no mortgage to pay off debt. How clever.

d. Buy Some Time to Get Back on Your Feet

Plenty of people may have gone into foreclosure because they have lost their job, run out of money, borrowed more money that they can pay back, went through some form of depression, or are going through a divorce or illness. Whatever the reason is, if you are facing foreclosure, it would be wise to buy some time and live rent free. If you can buy some time, then just maybe you will be able to overcome the hurdle that got your into foreclosure the first place. Perhaps you have lost a job, and if you stay rent free for a couple months, a new job will come about and you will be able to start paying on the loan again. Buying time can also help you to land back on your feet. Read the following scenarios and tell me which one sounds better to you:

In January 2009, Janie Smith lost her job and she could not make her mortgage payment. After 90 days of not making a mortgage payment, the lender initiated foreclosure proceedings. Janie Smith, without a job, mailed the keys back to the lender, and then she went to rent. Without a job, she was not able to pay her rent and she got evicted.

Pat Brown, in January 2009, lost her job and she could not make her mortgage payment. After 90 days Pat Brown's bank began foreclosing on her home. Pat Brown however, with no job, decided that she would not leave her home until she got back on her feet. So she bought a book on foreclosure and got familiar with everything she needed to know on foreclosure, and she used the tactics from the foreclosure book to fight the bank. Because of this, Pat Brown was able to stay in her home rent free for 10 months. During the 10 month phase, she got a job, was able to save money and was able to pay off credit card bills. Then she went to rent after the foreclosure took place.

Based upon both scenarios, which one would you rather be in? I hope you say Pat Brown. Because, as you can tell, someone who lives rent free has the privilege of paying off debt. Someone who lives rent free has the privilege of saving money. Someone who lives rent free has the privilege of perhaps not being too stressed out about meeting too many bills. After all, if your mortgage or rent payment is the largest debt for you to meet monthly, imagine if you no longer have to pay for it. You could save a lot. So if you ever go into foreclosure, please remember to consider the option of living rent free, and that my give you a chance of paying some debt off.

6.   Laws Change in Your Favor
I have been practicing foreclosure law for over a while. I started my experience during law school and my career has just been enriched with helping homeowners save their homes. One thing I can tell you that is fascinating about foreclosure is that the law keeps changing. And because the laws keep changing, well, homeowners who hold on to their

homes, can find themselves getting some form of favor, as congress and President Obama become sympathetic toward these homeowners' needs. So what am I saying? I am telling you if you are facing foreclosure, it is not always a bad thing. In fact, you can rest assured today being in foreclosure is a good thing.

For one thing, the fact that over 7 million Americans will face foreclosure in the year 2011 means that perhaps either all these Americans are dead beats, or all these Americans have been sold a really horrible product by their greedy lender.

Next, the fact that 7 million Americans will face foreclosure means these Americans have the power to get the law to change. All it takes is their voice, their advocates and a group of strong leaders in foreclosure advocating to their congressman and congresswoman the unfair treatment the homeowners obtained from the greedy lenders.

Let me explain a little about American politics based upon what I have learned from being an attorney who has made a few politicians my friends. Politicians love to be voted in. And they can only get voted in by their constituents, the people who reside in their district, or constituency. You may not believe it, but it is still the truth; the politicians really work for the people and when there is an election cycle, any politicians who desire to be in office will try to impress the people who voted them in. Now if all the people who voted them in or a majority of people that voted them in are losing their homes, do you think that politician would want to help them? You bet they will. Do you know why? Because the politicians want to make the voters happy so that the voters will keep voting them in office. Now if a voter is losing his home and the politician didn't do anything to help this voter save the home, the politician did not stop it. The politician did not advise the voter what to do about saving the home. The politician did not try to pass laws that would force the banks to work with troubled borrowers. The politician just did nothing. Do you think the voter would like the politician to keep staying in office? Probably not. And politicians, or the people who get politicians in office, do research and they know what topics are near and dear to the voters. A very hot topic for the coming years will be the housing market. No one can escape that. Foreclosure is predicted to be a norm in America for the next three years. And even though it is a norm, people do not like losing their homes. It is the duty of politicians to do something about it. Politicians are supposed to curb the greed of the banking institutions. After all, the people have no power to jail the CEOs of banks and the other executives that run them. But the politicians do. So the voice of the people is vested in the politicians and the system only works when the politicians hear the voice of the people and act upon it.

I must say, now that a vast majority of Americans are facing foreclosure, it really does appear that the government has put a few, not a lot, but a few measures in to place so that Americans can save their homes. So this is why it is very important for a person to hold on to her foreclosure home. Imagine you are in foreclosure and you are able to stall it and while you are stalling it, some very favorable law that will help you get to keep your home, gets passed. Wouldn't that just make your day? You would be able to keep your home.

But imagine if you are in foreclosure and you just walk away from the home and then you went to pay rent on a property that you hate very much. While you are paying high rent, you are not able to save any money. To add insult to injury, a law passes that benefits homeowners in foreclosure. You will not be able to benefit from that law, because you walked away from your home. I think you would not be too happy because had you stalled the foreclosure, help would come to you. There is an old saying that must be true. God helps those who help themselves. I hate to be the bearer of this news, but you better look out for yourself. There is no government, no entity, no career—nothing that will look out for you. You probably love yourself more than anybody can love you. And if you do, only you know what is best for you. If you are still in foreclosure, do what you can to hold on to your home. It will be worth it in the long run.

7. *Over Time Everything Changes*

When I had just started foreclosure, this cycle around 2005, I noticed that the lenders were very, very aggressive. I also noticed the demeanor of the judges. The judges ruled against the defenses being raised. I also noticed that it was really hard, in fact, close to impossible, to sign up clients in foreclosure. Foreclosure attached a stigma. Telling people I defend foreclosures was like telling them that I had the world's most contagious disease. It felt uncomfortable. But I had such a conviction that I stuck to my guns and I kept representing homeowners in foreclosure even with the stigma. Even my law peers refused to associate with me. Some of them even questioned my judgment and someone them thought I had for sure lost my mind and I was heading off a cliff sometime soon. I had such a burning desire to start a major foreclosure clinic and I had a vision that it would help millions of Americans save their homes. The problem is that, in 2005, there was not much foreclosure and millions of Americans were not losing their homes. And even if they were, they were just not coming forward for help.

But, I had overviewed a loan from a single lady around age 32, who holds a Ph.D. in psychology. When I saw what the loan looked like I was just beyond myself. A bulb went off inside my head. But not only that, I thought to myself, if this very intelligent woman signed this loan, what did others who had no Ph.D. do? If the bankers could sell this to the very intelligent, what have they sold to the masses? I knew the result would be ugly. And I knew the cry would be great. And I knew people would come for help because they would find out that the banks screwed them over. So the first few years in foreclosure were horrific. Because of the stigma attached to foreclosure, it was just unbearable. I could barely get the clients to come forward. The clients I forced into my law firm expressed guilt, embarrassment, pride and stress. They kept thinking they deserved to lose their homes because they missed a mortgage payment. The clients could not understand that maybe predatory lending should be blamed. Maybe the bank had no intention of them holding on to the home. Maybe if 7 million people are losing their homes, maybe something is just wrong and it had nothing to do with the borrower. It had to do with the bank trying to generate millions of dollars of fees and sell to China, a booming population. And in order for the banks to sell to China, well, they needed a pawn, and that pawn became a hardworking American who trusted the bank. And just maybe karma pays off. Maybe the banks are beginning to get a taste of their own medicine when homeowners facing foreclosure fight back (which unfortunately is only 5% of the total population fighting back). In any event, how cool is that?

Over time everything changes. The demeanor of society, the judges, the attorneys, and the people handling foreclosure in 2005 was very different from what it is today. I find that the judges are being more understanding to a homeowner. There are more attorneys fighting foreclosure today than there were in 2005, which means there are many more resources for people. The realtors working on short sales are becoming more experienced in handling foreclosures. The entire foreclosure system is changing in terms of the stigma being removed. So the longer you stay in foreclosure, the better it will be. Maybe someday foreclosure will no longer be a problem. Maybe there will be so many more experts working in the field that a foreclosure will be a five-minute issue for you to handle. So stay in your home as long as you can. As things change for the better, more options will become available causing you to keep your home. If you leave your home, then when the options become available it will be too late for you to benefit from them.

A homeowner in a non-judicial state may be able to stall time by doing the following things:

1. Short Sale.
2. Loan Modification Work Out.
3. Deed in Lieu.
4. Bankruptcy.

Since this chapter is only limited to judicial foreclosure, we will now discuss the pleadings and what they mean: How to read them, which ones are important, what to do with them, what to look out for, and, at minimum, what to file to stall the foreclosure and how to get in front of a judge or a mediator.

The Complaint.
The plaintiff usually files the complaint. A lawsuit generally involves two party. The plaintiff (the person who sues) and the defendant (the person who is being sued). If the lender sues you, then you become the defendant. The lender may list other defendants, but that may not be of any concern to you. If you live in an association, the lender will list the

association as a defendant. If you owe the IRS some money, and the IRS puts a lien on your home, then the plaintiff will list the IRS as a defendant. If you have any judgments against you and it is recorded in the public records of the county you reside in, or it is a record against your home, then those judgments will be defendants also. If you took out a second loan against the property, then that second loan will also be a defendant (unless of course, the second lender initiates the foreclosure). If you purchased the home with a spouse and the spouse signed the deed or mortgage, then that spouse will be a defendant.

The complaint also lists in numbers and paragraphs a story it tells to the court. In that story, the complaint outlines to the court that the court has jurisdiction to hear the case. It tells the court why. The court may have jurisdiction to hear the case because you are probably a resident living in the state where the court is or the property is more than likely in the county where the court is located. The complaint also tells the court the story of what is causing the dispute and what needs to be done in order to correct the dispute. Generally speaking, in a foreclosure, the only thing that causes the dispute is that you didn't pay the mortgage and the bank is requesting the court to grant them permission to sell the home so the bank can satisfy the mortgage term.

What Is a Summary Judgment and Why on Earth Is the Bank Requesting One?
Once the bank serves you and if there are other defendants, it serves them too. It will do some crazy move. It will first count down the days to seek a motion for default. This means if you or the other defendant have not responded to the lawsuit within the time the court gives (20 days), then the bank will ask the clerk of the court to default you, which means you will be barred from defending the lawsuit. Once the clerk grants the default, the bank will then file for summary judgment. The bank is basically saying, everything in the complaint is true and now the judge should agree and grant the bank permission to sell the home and in certain

cases, grant the bank permission to obtain a Deficiency Judgment (if the lender requested it in the complaint). Since a default defendant is much easier to obtain, the bank will just put together a few affidavits to prove its case. This includes an affidavit that states the amount owed and the bank's attorney will want to get attorney fees, so it too will provide an affidavit as to fees. Once this is done, the bank will then set its summary judgment for hearing. Once the summary judgment hearing gets completed, the judge will usually grant the bank permission to sell the home perhaps at least 30 days from the date it obtained the judgment.[20]

If you want to follow along on your foreclosure, you can track the case number by going on line to your county public records. Or you can call the clerk of court for your county providing her with your case number and she will tell you the last pleadings filed in your case. That way, if you do not hire an attorney at minimum you will know the time line on when the property will be sold at a public auction.

---

20 This is an illustration of the time line in the State of Florida. Please check your state Statute which will outline the accurate time line for a Summary Judgment and all foreclosure proceeding.

Chapter 10
Monitoring Your Foreclosure Lawsuit in the Court System and Deciding When to File Pleadings to Stall for Time

Reasons to Ride out Foreclosure

Well, if you are unable to afford an attorney, and you decide that you will ride out your foreclosure. Your reason may be to save money. Your reason may be because you are hopeful that the law will change in your favor. Your reason may be because you have small children who need to attend a school where the foreclosure home is located. Your reason may be because you feel like a victim of a scheme of Wall Street meltdown. If you have a pulse and you are living in America in the year 2010, then you may be listening or reading the news on what is going on on Wall Street. It will come as no surprise that most homeowners who are facing foreclosure may just be victims of predatory lending. So with that in mind, you should feel entitled to live in your place rent-free, rather than mail the keys to the lender. So let us say you reach a point, where you decide rent free is for you, but at the same time you cannot afford to hire an attorney to defend your foreclosure, then you still need to have a timeline.

Why Do You Need a Timeline?

In the judicial states, when you entered into a default under your mortgage, an uncontested foreclosure can be completed as little as three months. This means if you do not contest your foreclosure, then from the date you got served to the date you have to move can be as little as three months. Remember, what is happening in foreclosure. You are losing the title to your property and a court is going to grant the lender the home. You cannot legally stay in your home after the auction because the new owner will request that the sheriff remove you and your belongings. Once you lose your home at the public auction, then the title will pass from you to someone else (usually the lender or the successful bidder at the public auction). So at the point, you have no more rights to live in the home. You become a trespasser at that point. You do not want to end up going home one day to see your belongings thrown on the roadside. So don't be scared. It won't happen to you, if you are able to monitor the foreclosure. By monitoring the foreclosure, you will have a road map of just when the sale date will occur. Once the sale date occurs, at that point, you need to move out, unless of course, you hired a skilled foreclosure attorney who can delay the foreclosure even longer. Or of course, you file for bankruptcy protection. (For more on bankruptcy, see chapter 5).

Can I Call the Lender to Provide Me with the Road Map and Sale Date on My Home Rather than Hire an Attorney or Do the Search Myself?

Most homeowners really do not understand that once you stop paying on your mortgage, the lender no longer cares about you. Most homeowners are very naive about this. When I counsel homeowners facing foreclosure, I am surprised to see just how naive they are about the greedy lender. I had a potential client walk away from my office after I told her not to trust the lender. She contacted the lender who promised to advise her on when the property would be up for sale. That lender lied to her. And the poor potential client ended up losing her home even before the sale date took place. By losing her home prior to the sale, that potential client was forced to rent a property and she was not able to enjoy the benefit of living rent free and saving. The lender really has an incentive to hide the truth from you. The lender is losing money. It does not want a homeowner to be living in the home rent free. So if you are that naive to think that a bank is going to help you determine the timeline for you to lose your property, you have something else coming. At most the bank will deter you from staying in the premises rent free. And the bank will either force you to sell the property or move out. Or they will force you to sign new documentation which will waive your right to sue them for all the liability that you may have against them in foreclosure. I mean, face it. Most homeowners in foreclosure probably have valid claims against the lender for predatory lending, fraud, securitized pooling and servicing agreement. Most lenders do not even own the note they attempt to foreclosed on. The lender will always tell you not to hire an attorney because the lender wants to screw you. And the lender does not want you to screw it. Why do you think CEOs of banks make that much money? It is a simple fact. What you do not know will make you poor. And the banks know this.

Homeowner Monitoring Foreclosure

Okay, so let us say you have read this book and you have developed the confidence to monitor your own foreclosure and to file a few pleadings with the court to delay it. Congratulations. You have guts and you have got to feel good about not being bullied by the big corporate banks who think every homeowner who faces foreclosure is a wimp. You have got to feel good about the fact that you have the power to string along greedy banks who are so used to getting everything they want by a couple of calls. After all, banks are very powerful entities and you are just a normal human being. But you know, it usually is that normal human beings end up doing extraordinary stuff. And I think if at least 20% of homeowners in foreclosure can put up a fight, even if they end up losing their home, just maybe Wall

Street will begin to recognize that poor people have had enough. And fighting for your home in foreclosure will be worth it in the long run. Think about the money you can save by living rent free. Think about another bragging story that you can share with your neighbors or others who were not as lucky. You will look like a king or queen to others who just ran away without even thinking twice. And with this tough recession, you will have money in your bank account and you can perhaps ride out the credit crunch.

What a Homeowner Needs to Know in Judicial Foreclosure about Pleadings

Although I am attorney, I am not helping you to practice law. Keep in mind: This book is merely education. So please do not think that I am helping you in the practice of law. I want to tell you what each document means. That way, you kind of have an idea about the stages of foreclosure.

Foreclosure Stages
Default

Usually when a homeowner has not paid her mortgage payment for over 30 days, the lender will look at it as a default occurred. Some lenders will initiate foreclosure 30 days after the default. But it seems to be common practice that lenders wait for around 90 days of default before they initiate foreclosure.

Acceleration

In order for the lender to foreclose on the home, the lender has to accelerate the debt. What this means is even though you have not made a mortgage payment for let's say 90 days, in your mind, you might say, well I only owe three months which is let's say $1000 per month on a payment. So you are thinking who will foreclosure for $3000.00? But that is not the case. What the lender does is call the note. By doing so, they are not requesting that you pay the $3000.00. It is requesting that you pay the bank back the entire amount of the mortgage amount. So let us say you borrowed $100,000 and you had been making payments for five years. Your loan balance is $95,000.00. However, you have not made three months of mortgage payments, which is 3000.00. The lender will accelerate the loan balance of $95,000 and you will be getting a letter from the lender or the lender's attorney asking you for the $95,000, plus interest, fees and other costs.

Summons and Complaint

Once the lender identifies your loan as a default loan, then the next step is to either accelerate the debt or the lender's attorney will accelerate the debt. Then there is a waiting time of around 30 days. But you may get more, depending how slow the bank or the attorney moves. That 30 day window tells you to pay the amount owed or work on other ways to satisfy the debt. Once that window of opportunity expires, a homeowner can expect a process server or a sheriff to be knocking at the door. And it is not to greet you with warm wishes. Rather it is to hand you a summons and complaint. The process server or sheriff will identify who he is and he will tell you that you are being served and you have 20 days to respond to the lawsuit. Then he will write some information on there. (Usually that information is the date and time that you got served.) That way, the court and the lender's attorney and you will know when you 20 days begin.

If you decide to take the route of hiring an attorney, then make sure you hire an attorney within that 20 days. That way, the attorney can defend the foreclosure. If you decide to monitor the foreclosure, then do nothing with the paper, aside from take the case number down and the style of the case. The style of the case tells you who the plaintiff is and who the defendants are. There might be more than a few defendants. But you need to know this information because that is how you will track the case, from the time the complaint has been given to you, until the time the sale date will occur. If you decide to play a little legal lee, then you will need to get a form book on pro se defense. A form book on pro se defense will help you maneuver the court house. At best it will help you to delay the foreclosure. You can also look for foreclosure forms, but make sure it is in line to the state and county that you are in. A pro book or other forms may, however, not help you to delay the fore-closure the way an attorney can do it. Face it. An attorney is more of a pro. They went to school to get the training and they do it almost every day, which leaves them with above-normal skills. It is like cooking a meal or eating out at a five star restaurant with a fancy chef. You will be able to taste the difference in food. But I understand, some people just do not have the money to pay a lawyer. So work your way through with the form books. You will need to focus on two to three pleadings.

Motion to dismiss
Within the 20 days of the lawsuit, you must file with the court and a copy to the opposing side a Motion to Dismiss the case. Your motion to dismiss will go in line with something like the following.

Here are a very few ideas on a motion to dismiss:

1.   Improper Service
This just says that the plaintiff did not obtain the proper service of the complaint. Let us say that your 10-year-old daughter answered the door and the process server handed her the lawsuit to give to you. Then that would be an improper service.

2.   Failure to Join an Indispensable Party
This just means that the lawsuit may have some defective information in it that will cause the bank not to obtain the property. Let us say that you purchased your home with your best friend, Rick James. As we all know, Rick is a super-freak. Let us say that Rick James and you are both on the mortgage and the title. However, the lawsuit reads in error that the property is owned by you only. Then that would be a cause to get the lawsuit dismissed because since you and Rick James purchased the property and signed on the

mortgage, then the lender must foreclose on both interests, which is you and Rick James. By not naming Rick James, the lender will not be able to obtain the foreclosure. As such, the lender will have to go ahead and start over.

3. Failure of a Condition Precedent

Pretend like the bank never ever wrote to you to tell you that you owe the money. You were never put on notice. Then you would file a motion to dismiss and the reason would be failure to meet a condition precedent because you must be put on notice that you are in default before the bank can go forward with the lawsuit.

Answer and Affirmative Defense

Once the lawsuit is filed and if you decide within the 20 days to file a Motion to Dismiss, you must wait for your Motion to Dismiss to be heard. Once it is heard, the judge will either grant it or deny it. If you are denied the Motion to Dismiss, and you want to keep the foreclosure going, then you must file an answer and affirmative defenses within perhaps five days from the date the Motion to Dismiss was denied. If you do not file within that time, your will lose your defense and it is likely that the plaintiff will move the foreclosure on a lot more quickly.

An answer just says you admit or deny each allegation in the complaint. By admitting the allegations, you are agreeing with the lender. By denying the allegation, you are disagreeing with the allegations that the lender's attorney states in its complaint. Word from the wise. If you want the lender to have to prove its case, I suggest that you deny a few if not all of the allegations in the complaint. That way, the lender will have a tougher time proving its case.

Motion for Mediation

If you decide to go pro se, you want to file a motion for mediation. But keep in mind, you cannot file a motion for mediation if you defaulted. You can, but it may be more difficult to obtain. So you want to file your motion to dismiss and/

or your answer, affirmative defenses prior to the summary judgment. Request a mediation. For a sample of a motion for mediation, please review the appendix of this book.

What Is a Mediation?

If you are facing foreclosure in a judicial state, it would be wise to file a motion for mediation. Mediation is not done by the judge, but rather a third neutral party, who is authorized to conduct the mediation. Mediation means that two parties that are in a dispute (you, and the bank in the foreclosure) come together to a third neutral party to come up with a way to settle this dispute. This would be a very good tool for a borrower facing foreclosure because the lender would be sending staff with the power to settle your foreclosure situation. One of the tough things in resolving your foreclosure issue is getting a person from the bank that has the power to resolve the issue. There is really very little disadvantage to mediation. Everything during mediation is kept confidential so even if a settlement is not reached, the parties do not have to worry about what is being said being used in court.

Default Judgment versus Summary Judgment

There will be two types of judgment that the lender seeks. This will depend on the status of the borrower. If a borrower does not respond within the 20 days from the date of service, then the lender's attorney will request a default. That way, the default will bar the borrower from raising any legal defenses. So let us say that your little daughter, who is 10, answers the door and accepts the complaint and summons. Let us say you did not raise that defense. You just say, oh look. My little daughter answered the door and she got served. And you did nothing, then even though that is a wrong way of serving you, the lender will still default you and move on. It will not be the lender's duty to correct its mistake. It would be the defendant's. Once the default is entered, it is very rare that the defendant can overturn it. Of course, you can always hire an attorney who may get it overturned.

In the motion for summary judgment, the lender's attorney will state a few allegations. The lender's attorney will just confirm that there is no reason to go to trial. If you have not responded to the lawsuit, this will even be better for the lender's attorney. The lender's attorney will point out to the court the date you got served. The fact that after 20 days you did not respond. And because you did not respond., the lender's attorney will request a default because you never responded to the lawsuit. And, of course, the lender's attorney will point out that there is no reason for them not to get the property and sell it. You owe the money and you did not raise any defenses that would put reasonable doubt or that would require a trial. If you do respond, the lender's attorney will still file for a motion for summary judgment. It will just tell the court that you responded. But your responses are not legal defenses or they are not defenses that should be heard at trial. Other words, you raised meritless defenses. And because of that, the lender's attorney should sell the property. However, keep in mind the difference with a default summary judgment and a summary judgment not on default, is a difference in months for delay. The person who raises defenses will have the lender working a little harder in proving its case. The person who did nothing, will let the lender get the property a lot quicker. So even if the court stricken down your defenses, still raises them. That may give you an extra 90 days, which, if your home is 1000 per month, then that is 3000.00 savings. Not bad for a tough recession.

What Happens at the Summary Judgment Hearing

If you have not filed any paperwork, then the bank's attorney will request that a default gets entered against you. So whatever the lender requested in the complaint, its attorney will argue at the summary judgment hearing that you are not disputing any issues so to go ahead and give the bank what the bank requested in the complaint. The bank made simple request. The bank's attorney would want the judge to agree that the bank is owed the money due under the mortgage or the complaint. The bank's attorney is entitled to legal fees for bringing the foreclosure to court. The bank is entitled to sell the property to satisfy the money that is owed from the mortgage (generally speaking that was the deal that a homeowner and a bank cut when at closing). You probably don't remember much because every homeowner gets excited about purchasing her home. During the purchase of a home, most homeowners do not have the money to buy a home so they usually borrow the money from a bank. The lender eagerly lends the money. In order to lean the money, the lender gets the homeowner to sign a mortgage, which says that if the homeowner refuses to pay, then the lender will call the loan (acceleration) and then the lender will foreclosure on the mortgage. So the summary judgment just summarizes what the lender and the borrower agreed to. But since the borrower is in a judicial state, then a judge will have to sign off on the lender's request to call the mortgage and foreclosure.

Unlike an evidentiary hearing or trial, a summary judgment hearing usually lasts for less than five minutes. Moreover, the lender's attorney proves the lawsuit through sworn affidavits. Uncontested summary judgment last around two minutes. As a previous foreclosure attorney, I know exactly what is said at the hearing.

The lender's attorney usually just tells the judge the defendant's name, the bank's name, the date the defendant made the last mortgage payment, the amount owed to the bank and then a request to sell the property on behalf of the bank. Once the judge okays it, then the lenders attorney will hand the judge the paperwork. And the case gets closed because the paperwork that the judge signs off on usually involves the lender getting a sale date for the property and a writ of possession, which allows either the lender or the new owner to remove the previous owners.

A sale date usually is anywhere from 30 days after the summary judgment hearing to 120 days after the summary judgment hearing. However, with the new filings on the internet, the sale date may be a lot quicker. And I suspect that is for all judicial states with the filing of an online auction.

In any event, if you are in a judicial state, you will know the sale date by monitoring your foreclosure. You monitor your foreclosure by checking with the clerk of the court in the county the property is located. Some are online and others are in person. Once you have the case number and the style of your case, you must keep calling or checking online to see the progress of the case. It will provide you with a road map which will help you to come up with the date to move out of the home, prior to be thrown out of the house.

If you are not organized and diligent in performing these searches, then hire a foreclosure attorney who has the tools effective to monitor the case. That way, you will at least get a 30-120 day notice on when to move.

Basic Foreclosure Defense
Below, this information will cover homeowners who live in a judicial state. If you have decided to move forward on your own foreclosure defense, this information below will just explain a few defenses that can be used. Again, this book is not intended to substitute the use of an attorney. I would highly suggest that you retain a foreclosure or real estate attorney in your jurisdiction.

The following defenses are based upon common law, property law and federal statutes. Once a complaint is served, a homeowner has 20 days to respond. Usually the homeowner would file a motion to dismiss. In the motion to dismiss, the homeowner will state the Plaintiff has done one of the following:

1. The court lacks personal jurisdiction over the subject matter.
2. The plaintiff fails to state a cause of action for which relief can be granted.
3. The plaintiff fails to join an indispensable party.

4. The plaintiff lacks standing to sue.
5. The plaintiff has violated the Federal Fair Debt Collection Practices Act.
6. Improper service.
7. The Plaintiff has failed to meet a condition precedent in bringing forth the lawsuit.

Once the dismissal is heard, the judge will either deny the defendant's motion to dismiss or grant it. If the judge denies the defendant's motion to dismiss, the judge will allow the defendant to respond to the complaint within 10 to 20 days from the date the order was issued.[21] Below is a roadmap on the foreclosure tactic:

1. File an answer and affirmative defenses.
2. The answer would usually state:
   a. admit,
   b. deny or
   c. without knowledge.
3. The affirmative defenses that may be used for a foreclosure defense are as follows:

   1. Lost note.
   2. Illegal charges added to the balance.
   3. Predatory lending.
   4. Estoppell/wavier.
   5. Failure to join an indispensable party.
   6. Unjust enrichment.
   7. Plaintiff has not posted a bond for bringing the claim.
   8. Plaintiff lacks standing.
   9. Plaintiff is in violation of the Federal Fair Debt Collection Practices Act.
   10. Duress.
   11. Fraud.
   12. RICO Violation (see your state statue to see what statutes covers Rico Violation).

---

21 This information is based on time line in State courts in Florida. Please check your state Statute for accuracy.

13. Violation of Truth in Lending Act, TILA (16 U.S.C Section 1601).
14. Violation of Real Estate Settlement Procedural Act RESPA (12 U.S.C. Section 2601).
15. Violation of Homeownership Equity Protection Act, HOEPA (16 U.S.C. Section 1639).
16. Unconscionability.
17. Unfair and Deceptive Fair Trade Practice.
18. Failure to accelerate the loan.
19. Failure to service the mortgage in accordance with HUD.
20. Action is bared by the Statute of Frauds (if applicable).
21. Payment.
22. Right of Recession.
23. Plaintiff has failed to notify Defendant within 30 days of an assignment of mortgage (if applicable).
24. Forced placed insurance is added to the balance.
25. Unclean hands.

For sample pleadings, please check the appendix. Additionally, you will need to tailor the pleadings to fit your needs.

Chapter 11
Save Your Home through Refinance or Short Pay-Off Refinance

If you want to save your home from foreclosure, you may have to refinance the loan. A refinance occurs when you pay off your old mortgage with a new mortgage. However, in order to refinance your home, you must have enough equity in your home. Equity means that your house is worth more than your mortgage amount. If you are upside down on your mortgage payment, then a traditional refinance will not be an option because most banks will only allow you to refinance a loan if you have enough equity in your property. The equity will be used to pay off the existing loan and you will be taking out a new loan during the refinance.

Do not despair, if you lack equity in your property. The Obama Administration will save the day. Part of what the Obama administration enacted is a loan modification program called HOPE. According to that plan, many troubled borrowers with no equity in their property will be able to refinance their homes. The government provides specific guidelines for it. For more information, please see the chapter on loan modification. For now, this chapter deals with a refinance, in which the borrower has equity in her home.

But then again, these days are different. So my advice is for you to check with your lender to see if the government-enacted special programs to help troubled borrowers will work for you if you have no equity. We are in a national crisis in the housing market. And because of that, it is likely that the government has made some special programs available for troubled borrowers who have homes with no equity to refinance.

How to Refinance Your Home

Assume that you have enough equity in your home, but you are a troubled borrower. So let us say you are about to face foreclosure as you took on a loan that is adjustable (meaning the interest rate is about to go higher, which means the monthly payment will be more than what it is on your home now). If you can take out a new loan with the same bank or another bank and the payments will be cheaper, then you can refinance your way out of foreclosure. In order to refinance it is important that the borrower come to terms with a few things. Below is what the borrower needs to do in order to obtain a refinance:

1. Contact your current lender to see if they can offer you a refinance.
2. Either do the work on your home, by shopping for a loan or use a mortgage broker. The advantage of using a mortgage broker is that the broker will be able to shop many loans at the same time.
3. Get an appraisal on your property. That way, you know what the value is on the property and the amount of equity in the property. Equity is the difference between what the property is worth and what the loan amount is. If it is negative equity, then a traditional refinance will not work. You will need a short pay-off refinance (see Page 103 on short pay-off refinance).
4. Shop around, so that you can obtain cheaper payments. Banks may vary on their loan product. The key is to save as much as you can. So if you are preapproved from one bank, go to others to see what loan terms and what payments they have to offer you.
5. Review your current mortgage to see if there is a prepayment penalty. If a prepayment penalty is on the note,

then that would be money that will be forked up at the new closing (remember, a refinance is same as taking out a mortgage, so you will have to close).

6. Get a free copy of your credit report. You want to check to make sure your credit report is accurate, because this may help with you getting a good mortgage or a not so good one.

7. Have your documentation ready to go. The lender will require your recent bank statements, tax returns, pay stubs, and other paperwork.

Is Refinancing Right for You?
Keep in mind, this book details foreclosure defense and how to save your home from foreclosure. Refinance will be right for you if you get to save your home. Below are the reasons you should refinance the loan if you are able to.

   1. *Cheaper payments*
      Pretend that Sally Johnson has an adjustable mort-gage. She took out a loan some time in 2005 and she obtained the teaser rate. A teaser rate is when the payments are low at first, and then they get ridicu-lously high. Pretend, Sally has a good job and she has equity in her home. Her adjustable rate is about to jump higher. Her interest rate will go from 7% to 14%, which means her monthly payments will for sure dou-ble. Sally will not be able to afford the home, once the interest rate hits 14%. As such, Sally is left with a few choices. She can sell the home and walk away. Or she can refinance the home and get a cheaper payment. Sally should then refinance the home if she plans on living there a couple more years. You see, once Sally refinances, then she can get another loan that is back to 7% or less. That way, Sally will get to save her home. So in this situation, refinance would be wise, since for sure, Sally will get a cheaper payment.

2. *Save your home from foreclosure*

Refinancing is right for you if it will save your home from foreclosure. Pretend, Tom Jones purchased a home back in 2005 and he now has equity in there. Tom Jones is about to face foreclosure because his mortgage payments will jump high because he took out a teaser rate. Jones should then refinance the loan to be saved from foreclosure. His only way to save the home is through a refinance.

3. *You qualify for a new mortgage*

If you must save your home by a refinance, the payments are cheaper and you qualify for a new loan, then by all means, refinance is for you. Chaser Bank owns a loan for Jerry Brown. Jerry Brown needs to refinance because Chaser gave Jerry Brown an adjustable mortgage. The teaser rate on that adjustable mortgage is about to jump higher, which means Brown's payment will be higher. Jerry Brown decides to call Chaser to obtain a new loan. Chaser agrees to help him, but Chaser decides since it is a new loan Brown must still qualify. Jerry Brown applies and does not get the new loan. Brown believes because he was already a customer of Chaser that Chaser would just give him a new mortgage. That is not the case. In order to obtain a new mortgage, the lender will generally require you to complete paper work, which means the only way you can refinance is if you qualify for it and that is regardless of the fact that you are using the same lender that has your current mortgage.

4. *You get out of that adjustable loan and now you are in a fixed rate*

Tom Brown purchased a home in 2005 and he obtained an adjustable loan. When Tom purchased the home, he was not sure if he would live in there for more than three years. So at the time, Tom took out an adjustable rate mortgage. Now Tom has been in the house for three years, he really fell in love with it. His kids are in a good school in that neighborhood and the home fits his lifestyle as it is close to restaurants, parks, local church, and everything that Tom loves. It is even close to work, which helps reduce the stress of driving long hours. Tom decides he wants to keep the home. However, he cannot afford the adjustable loans, because he does not like the uncertainty of having a loan that he can afford for three years and then it jumps after that. As such, Tom decides he will refinance the loan because the new lender is offering him a fixed rate (fixed rate means that the principle and interest remain the same for the life of the loan). Tom figures with all the uncertainty in the economy, a fixed rate would be the only way he can keep the home. So Tom jumps on the refinance because the new loan offers Tom a fixed rate for the life of the loan.

Short Pay-Off Refinance
You might be saying to yourself that everything sure sounds good, except for one minor detail. You have no equity in your property. So does that mean you are out of luck? The answer is no. You are still in luck. Have you heard about the short pay-off refinance? Let me let you into a little secret. Most people do not know it exists. If they did, then they would not be losing their homes.

What Is a Short Pay-Off Refinance?
A short pay-off refinance is when a borrower is underwater with her mortgage. That means the loan on the property is more than what the property is worth. Usually a borrower will probably be a candidate for foreclosure because of equity deprivation. So prior to going into foreclosure, and with a decent credit score (anything above 650), the borrower can refinance her way out, by a short pay-off refinance.

What Is Required to Obtain the Short Pay Off?

A short pay is not a short sale. With a short sale, you lose the title to the home (see the chapter on Short Sale). This is different. With short pay-off refinance, you still have the home. It is still yours. However, a short pay-off is not right for everyone and not everyone will obtain a short pay-off refinance. Both the lender and the borrower must be on board. So it is one thing to have this information, but the borrower must convince the lender to accept the short pay off because it would be in the lender's best interest. Because by not accepting the short pay off, the homeowner may be heading to foreclosure soon. The following criteria must be met in order for a borrower to obtain a short pay off refinance:

1. Borrower must be current on the mortgage (so obtain the short pay off, before you default on the loan).
2. Borrower must have a decent credit score (it appears anything above 650 will be okay).
3. The borrower must have an income. And the income will be documented by taxes, profit and loss statements (if self-employed), pay stubs and bank statements.
4. The borrower's mortgage must be underwater, meaning you owe more on the mortgage than the property is worth.
5. The bank or loan servicers must be willing to accept a short pay-off. The borrower or the borrower's attorney or agent must convince the lender that a short pay-off is the most profitable for the lender; still the borrower may be facing foreclosure if the pay-off is not granted.

Below is an example

Pat James works hard as a sales person. Pat James' credit score is 680. Pat purchased his home in 2006 for $350,000.00. In, 2010, the property value plummeted to $150,000. Pat recently got a pay reduction, so he will not be able to keep up with the mortgage payment on a $350,000 loan mortgage. Pat loves the home, and Pat wants to save the home. So Pat decides to do a short pay-off refinance. Pat contacts his lender, Blue Bank, to explain of the mortgage crisis that he will face. Pat convinces his lender to accept a lesser amount for pay off. Blue Bank agrees. Pat then goes to the Pink Bank and Pink Bank agrees to loan Pat money on $150,000.00 (the current value on the home). At that point, Pat uses the $150,000 mortgage to pay Blue Bank. Blue Bank releases the mortgage from Pat's home. And the $200,000 that Pat owed to Blue Bank becomes a forgiveness of debt. Blue Bank 1099s Pat for the $200,000. Pink Bank then records a mortgage against Pat's home for the $150,000. Pat is able to save his home through the short pay-off refinance because the payments became affordable, now that he only has to pay a mortgage on $150,000.00.

FHA Short Pay-Off Refinance.
What if you lack the equity to do a traditional refinance, but you also do not have a great credit score, would there be another program out there? The answer is yes. If you qualify for an FHA short refinance, then you will be eligible for a new mortgage, which means that you would refinance your way from the higher mortgage amount to a lower mortgage amount. Of course, this in the long term means savings. For example, not only will you no longer be underwater with your mortgage, but you will also have a cheaper mortgage payment.

What Are the Requirements for an FHA Short Refinance:
1. A credit score of over 500.
2. The borrower must be underwater with his mortgage, meaning his property is worth less than the mortgage amount owed on the property.
3. The current lender must agree to let the borrower do a short pay off (you have to understand, that the current lender is taking less. Take for example you owe $300,000 on the mortgage. And the property is worth $100,000. Then the short pay-off means, you will be paying the lender $100,000 and the lender would have to write off

$200,000. So the trick will be to convince the lender to accept only $100,000 from you).

4. FHA will loan up to a 90% loan on the current value of your property. So you may or may not need a deposit down. You would have to convince the current lender to take less (but make sure the amount includes the 10% that FHA will not be able to accept. That way, you will not have to absorb that down payment).

5. You must be able to do a loan at full documentation. This means, you must provide your income, taxes, bank statements and recent pay stubs.

6. You must be able to qualify for the new mortgage amount. That means if the new mortgage amount is $100,000.00, then your gross income must be able to cover the monthly mortgage payment.

7. You must be current on your existing mortgage. That means, you would need to work on this program before you enter foreclosure and before you are late on your payment. Not after.

What Is A Home Affordable Refinance Program? (HARP)
What if I am a homeowner that has no equity in my property, can the homeowner still refinance her way out foreclosure? And the answer is absolutely. HARP (Like HAMP in Chapter 6) is a refinance program that will help homeowners who would not qualify otherwise for a refinance on their current home. However, your loan must be owned by Freddie Mac or Fannie Mae.

If you are not sure who the owner of your note is, you can do two things:

1. You can call your lender or the servicer of your loan and ask the lender or servicer of your loan whether Fannie Mae or Freddie Mac owns the note. (The information for your lender is given to you every month. If you have a mortgage and you are current, then you will be receiving a mortgage statement. In that statement, it tells you how much to pay each month. It also provides you with

various numbers to your lender or the servicer) When you call up your lender or servicer, be prepared to answer questions like your social security number and address. They only do that to verify who you are.

2. If you have access to the internet, then you can always look up the information by yourself. The web pages are below:
http://loanlookup.fanniemae.com/loanlookup/_
https://ww3.freddiemac.com/corporate/

How does HARP work?

So far, the HARP only covers your first mortgage. So HARP may not work for those with two loans attached to the property. If you obtained a loan through HARP, then the lender will refinance you up to 125% of your mortgage. So this is good news for homeowners who are underwater in their mortgage.

How Do I Qualify for HARP?

It appears that the following homeowners will be eligible for HARP:

1. Loan is a Fannie Mae, Freddie Mac.
2. You are underwater with your mortgage.
3. Your current interest rate is much higher than the prevailing market.
4. You suffered some form of hardship, which means you suffered from a loss of job, a decrease in income, a health issue or a divorce.
5. Your interest rate is about to adjust higher, which means you will not be able to afford the mortgage if the interest rate reset.
6. Must not have mortgage insurance on your current mortgage.

Why Would a homeowner Do a HARP?
Cheaper Payments

Pretend, things were going great for you, but because of the recession, your got laid off. You end up taking a job that pays at least $1000.00 per month less. Because of the job changes, you are having problems keeping up with your mortgage payment. You do not have any equity in your home, so a traditional refinance will not work for you. However, if your home mortgage is owned by a Fannie Mae or Freddie Mac, then you can try for the HARP. Once you obtain the HARP, you will receive cheaper payments. That may work out well for you, because now that your job income is less, you can still hold on to your home, because the payments are cheaper and now you can afford them.

Avoid Foreclosure

Let us say that your loan is going to go up from 6% to 14%. If the payment goes up to $400 extra per month, then you will probably go through foreclosure because the payment increase will not allow you to hold on to the mortgage. So if you are able to get the HARP, you will be able to perhaps lower your payment from 6% to 4%. So by saving the $400 per month, you will avoid foreclosure.

Chapter 12
Additional Resources

Once you read this book, you can also seek additional help on foreclosure defense and foreclosure alternatives. Over the years, I have seen organizations come on board to help homeowners facing foreclosure. Here are a few areas that you may want to obtain help from.

1. Non-profit organizations

You may want to seek a legal aid or other non-profit organization help like NAACA who help homeowners facing foreclosure. These organizations do not charge a fee because there are not for profit. I have heard feedback that since they are non-profit, that it is a little difficult to obtain help, because the waiting period may be a lot longer. But my advice is that you stay persistent and keep following up. You may also want to check with your local church. Some local churches have staff members that retired from the practice of law or account or retired business people. Based upon the previous profession that these church members were involved in, they will be able to provide you with help. Additionally, some attorneys or accountants who attend church may volunteer their time to help in finance and debt-free counseling. This may help with foreclosure as well. Based upon my experience, I noticed that many non-denominational churches stay current on various crises in their community. Since foreclosure is a major crisis for communities, churches perhaps already set up a local team to reach out to homeowners facing foreclosure.

2. *Professions- Lawyers, Accountants, Mortgage Broker and Realtors*

As mentioned in the book, you may need to hire a real estate or foreclosure attorney or bankruptcy attorney to help with your foreclosure situation.

3. *Internet and Libraries*

The internet has a wealth of information on foreclosure, short sale, short sale pay off and many things that are mentioned in this book. Just google or bing it and then add the words in there. This should help you to read a lot on the situation that you are facing.

If you still like to do things from scratch, then go to your local library and you can get help there. Just tell the librarian that you are looking for information on short sale, foreclosure, foreclosure defense and other information in this book. If you are more confident and savvy, then head to the courthouse and use the law library. Your local court house law library will provide a wealth of information on your state statutes and federal statutes. Those statutes will be very useful for your foreclosure defense or even if you need to know or become familiar with your legal rights, because you do have due process prior to losing property. So quickly become familiar with your rights because the bank is not going to tell you about your rights.

Another useful web page was designed by my Firm's foreclosure defense team. It helps residents in the Florida area. You can visit www.stopforeclosurenow-inflorida.com or www.foreclosuresurvivialguide.com

4. *Networking*

This may be one of the easiest and cheapest ways to get a wealth of information. Start talking to other people facing foreclosure. Avoid talking with your supervisor or your work peers, because this may be personal and you just do not want people at your job gossiping about your foreclosure dilemma. Additionally, you do not want your boss to fire you for taking time away from staff members to talk about your personal information. I am not promoting networking at the work area. Additionally you do not want your work rivals to have this information to use against you in case you are close to a promotion. At times, the work environment may view foreclosure and financial crisis as a weakness, and you truly never want to look weak in the work field. After all, employers hire people who add value to the company. However, there are other areas to network. Go to the local bar, start talking to strangers. Start eaves dropping when you are sitting down for dinner or lunch at a restaurant. You will be surprised to hear or listen in on how many people are facing foreclosure. Contact your neighbors and see if anyone is facing the same situation that you are facing. Gossip with your neighbors to find out who moved out of the area recently and what caused the move. If a neighbor left due to foreclosure, then contact that former neighbor to get information. Ask some key information. What happened? How did it happen? What did you learn from it? What could you have done better? What was the process like? How long did the foreclosure take? Get all the details and ask questions that will help you to overcome your foreclosure crisis. Call your family members and distant relatives and see if they are facing foreclosure or if they know of anyone facing foreclosure. You want to arm yourself with knowledge. Knowledge means power. And in this situation, what you do not know will rip the roof off your head. If you have children, then get to the school and try to meet other parents. Chit chat with them for a while and see if the foreclosure comes up. If not, try to bring it up to see if these parents know of someone who is in a similar situation. Use your social arena and dig for information. The key is to find someone with the same or similar experience. That way, you can draw information from them.

5.   *Contact Elected Officials at Local, State and Federal Levels*
Over the years, the political area has just been so much easier for citizens to reach out to their local officials. Through the internet, facebook, twitter, and other media attention, the officials are responding quickly. You may want to contact your state representative. The purpose of the contact is to see if he has any programs or any advice or can he steer you in the direction to help with your foreclosure situation. Additionally, if you have a lender that is abusing you in the foreclosure crisis, you want to write to your state representative, who can perhaps reach out and see to it that the lender is being investigated.

You want to write to your state attorney general as well and you want to call his office. The purpose would be to see if he has any information to help you on foreclosure. If of course, the foreclosure attorney or the lender is abusing your rights, you want to let the attorney general in your state know that. At times, lenders will change the lock on your door without even obtaining a court order. This is information that your attorney general needs to have, so he can document and go after your lender. Your attorney general may be able to help to steer you away from scam artist, as there are many corporations out there set up to scam you because of your vulnerable foreclosure situation.

During the election year, I noticed that the federal elected officials are very helpful in your foreclosure crisis. I know they may go beyond the call of duty just to help you in your foreclosure mess. If you are successful in obtaining help from your elected officials, they may even go as far as helping you obtain a loan modification, a forbearance or principle reduction. I read in a local paper that in 2010 Senator Harry Reid of Nevada ended up helping many homeowners obtain a loan modification. Prior to his involvement, the homeowners were unsuccessful in obtaining a loan modification. The lenders refused to accept their phone calls or the lenders were just mean and awful. Of course, you would need to know what district you are in and which elected official is assigned to your district. Then write and call. I cannot guarantee that it always work. But persistency pays off on this one. You may have better luck if you are writing or calling during an election cycle than not an election cycle.

Whether you are a republican or democratic or independent and you may not like your elected official because he or she is not the party you wanted in office or you did not vote for him or her, just put your pride behind you and still ask for help. You should also make sure your letter to an elected official is professional. Address the elected official as Congressman or Senator. You may also want to put some praises in there. Thank your elected official for the work he or she is doing, even if you do not agree. Avoid telling your elected official what a horrible job he or she has been doing, because remember you are trying to get your elected official to do something for you. Your letter should focus on some form of drama between you and your lender. I think the worst your situation looks, is the better opportunity you have of obtaining help from an elected official. If you are doing a strategic foreclosure, I would not put that in the letter nor would I think the elected official would respond to someone who just obtains a bad deal by buying real estate high, and you really have the money to pay for it but you choose not to because the property is not worth it. If you are a real estate investor that speculated on the foreclosure market, then I highly doubt that your elected official is going to help an investor who speculated on real estate to save his investment properties. If you are not too up with the law, like you are wanted in another state, or you fail to pay five years of taxes or you are involved something illegal, then even if you are in foreclosure, do not contact an elected official for help. Remember an elected official works for the government and you do not want to submit some paperwork to the elected official that may incriminate you in the end. I mean if you have not paid your taxes in five years and an elected official staff is required to help you with a modification, I strongly believe they would be calling IRS on you once you tell them you have not paid taxes in years. Please just use common sense.

If on the other hand, you own only one home. You recently lost your job. You are sick. You cannot get through to the bank. You pay your income taxes on time. You are a law abiding citizen. The bank calls and threatens you with bodily injury. The bank changes the lock on you just so you can leave and without going through the court system, if applicable. You are dirt poor or at the verge of bankruptcy. If you own one home, and you are losing it to foreclosure then that would be a plausible letter, but remember to add the drama. If children are involved, list their names, and ages, and how difficult it is for you to explain the situation to the kids. Once you write a letter to your politician, follow up by calling her office and speaking with one of her staff to see if your letter was received and what is the status. You will need to do some research by googling or binging your district, address for your elected officials, web pages and phone numbers. This area works. Lay people with no law degree, nor high school diplomas who have contacted elected officials for help will often receive help and follow up.

APPENDIX
(important forms and samples)
Sample Hardship Letter (loss of job example)

Sallie Brown
XXXX NE 5XXX Street
Fort Lauderdale, FL 33301

July 5, 2010

Mr. Dan Chin, Loss Mitigation Department
Bank of America
500 Sunshine Road
Boca Raton, Florida 33XXX

Re: Loan Number 189765-XXXX

Dear Mr. Chin:

My name is Sallie Brown. I live at XXXX NE XXX Street, Fort. Lauderdale, Florida, 33301. I have not made a mortgage payment since December 2009 because I did not have the money. I lost my job in December 2009. I have been living off my savings and borrowing from friends and family to make ends meet. The company that I worked for shut down. My boss told me that because of the recession, he was not able to keep all of us. I was then let go. I just got back another job and my first pay check comes in next week. Because of this job, I landed back on my feet and I want to save my home, even though I missed a few payments. I am sorry. Please work with me in obtaining a loan modification. I heard a loan modification means that you, the bank, will reduce my mortgage payment, so that it is cheaper and I will be able to make the monthly payment. Let me know what, if any, paperwork is needed. My contact information, such as my name and email address, is listed above. Please have someone call me and help me save my home. Thanks for reading this.

Sincerely,

Sallie Brown

Sample Hardship Letter (illness example)

Sallie Smith
XXXX NE 5ˣˣˣ Street
Fort Lauderdale, FL 33301

July 5, 2010

Mr. Dan Chin, Loss Mitigation Department
Bank of America
500 Sunshine Drive
Boca Raton, Florida 33XXX

Re: Loan Number 180065-XXXX

Dear Mr. Chin:

My name is Sallie Smith. I have not made a mortgage payment since November 2009, because I became sick. I had to address the sickness and an operation was necessary. As such, I missed a lot of time from work, which made my paycheck very little. It was not enough to cover all the bills. And the mortgage was the largest bill I had. And I could not make ends meet working very little hours and attending to my illness.

However, the sickness is gone and I just started working full time. I can prove to you that I can make the mortgage payment, by submitting to you the paystubs, and tax return, bank statements and all other necessary documents.

Please let me know what the next step will be. I want to save my home and I am truly sorry that my sickness caused me to work very little hours. But now that I am better, I am ready to work on saving the home.

You can reach me by telephone anytime at 561-939-XXXX. You can also email me at XXXXX@hotmail.com. You can also mail me directly at the house. I live there.

I look forward to hearing from you or someone who can help me save the home.

Thank you,

Sallie Smith

Sample Hardship Letter (divorce example)

Tanya Brown
XXX Spanish River Drive
Boca Raton, FL 33441

April 12, 2010

Mr. Dan James, Loss Mitigation Department
JC Mortgage Chase of America
500 Foreclosure Highway
New York, NY XXXXX

Re: Loan Number JCGREED180565-XXXX

Dear Mr. James:

I just called the bank and the bank told me to write to you about my hardship. I heard you want to know why I couldn't pay and by writing that will help me to get some form of help from the bank.

My name is Tanya Brown. My husband divorced me in December 2009 and he left the house. I used to depend on my husband's income as well as mine. Now that I am divorced, I fell behind on the mortgage payment because my husband was not able to give me his income anymore. I only get a very little and it only covers child support.

However, I do desire to save the home and have two solutions that will help me. I am planning on getting a second job. That way it can help me get the second income I need to make the mortgage payment. If that does not work, I am planning on renting one of my bedrooms and one of my bathrooms out. I will do so by getting a roommate. That way, a roommate will provide the additional income I need to cover the mortgage.

I already posted an ad for a roommate a week ago and have gotten plenty of responses. I also have been looking for a night job and have three job interviews line up for this week.

Both opportunities will truly allow me the time to get the second income I need to save the home.

Please mail me the paperwork that I need to save the home. My friend who saved her home said to request loan modification paperwork.

By the time I fill it out, I will have the additional income to make up for the mortgage.

My son and I love the house. The school system is really great here. I love my son going to school in this area. I am planning on staying here for the next 15 years. I want to raise my five-year-old here. So I will do what it takes to save the home.

Thank you for reading this letter.

Sincerely yours,

Tanya Brown

Sample Borrower's Financial Statement. The following financial statement is a sample of what you can expect to obtain from the lender, when you contact your lender to obtain a forbearance, a loan modification or a short sale.

Initials: _____

BORROWER'S FINANCIAL STATEMENT

Borrowers Name:
_____

Co-Borrowers Name:
_____

Property
Address: _____

_____

Lender: _____ Loan
Number: _____

Assets & Liabilities: If accounts are joint put figure in borrowers column and put joint in Co-Borrowers column

	Borrower:	Co-Borrower	Total
Liquid Assets			
Cash			
All Checking and Savings Accounts			
Stock/Bond/Mutual Funds/CD's			
401K			
Total Liquid Assets	$	$	$

Other Assets (Current Value)			
Primary Home			
Secondary Home / Any Other Property			
Automobile			
Make/Model/Year			
Make/Model/Year			
Cash Value of Life Insurance			
Personal Property (Comp/Furniture etc.)			
Total Other Assets			
TOTAL ASSETS:	$	$	$

	Borrower:	Co-Borrower	Total
Liabilities			
Existing 1st Mortgage on Subject Property			
Existing 2nd Mortgage on Subject Property			
Any other Mortgages			
Auto Loans			
All other Loans			
All Credit Cards			
Other:			
Other:			
TOTAL LIABILITIES:	$	$	$

X_____X_____

Borrowers Signature Co-Borrowers Signature Monthly Income	Borrower	Co-Borrower	Total
Employment Gross Salary			
Second Employment Gross Salary			
Rent a Room			
Self Employed Income			
Alimony-Child Support Income			
Personal Income Tax (Deductions %)			
Other:			
Other:			
TOTAL MONTHLY INCOME			
Monthly Expenses	Borrower	Co-Borrower	Total
Primary Home 1st Mortgage (P+I)			
Insurance			
Taxes			
HOA Fees			
Primary Home Mortgage Note 2			
Other Mortgages (Subject Property)			
Other Mortgages (Other Properties)			

Automobile Loan			
Automobile Loan			
Automobile Insurance			
Other Loans			
Credit Card (Minimum Payments All Cards)			
Alimony/Child Support/Child Care			
Utilities (water, electric, gas, cable etc.)			
Telephone (Land Line & Cellular)			
Insurance/Medical Expenses			
Groceries/Toiletries			
Transportation/Fuel			
Other:			
Other:			
TOTAL PERSONAL EXPENSES			
Monthly Income Less Expenses			
OTHER ITEMS NEED TO LIST:			
Property Taxes on Subject Property:			

X_____X_____

Borrowers Signature   **Co-Borrowers Signature**

Sample Motion to Dismiss

IN THE CIRCUIT COURT OF THE SEVENTEENTH JUDICIAL CIRCUIT OF THE STATE OF FLORIDA, IN AND FOR BROWARD COUNTY CIVIL DIVISION

ABC MORTGAGE CORPORATION

VS.   CASE NUMBER 10-65XXXX

JAMES HENRY, ET AL

_____/

DEFENDANT'S JAMES HENRY MOTION TO DISMISS PLAINTIFF'S COMPLAINT[22]

NOW INTO COURT, comes the Defendant James Henry (Hereinafter "**HENRY**"), and move that this Honorable Court Dismiss the Complaint filed by the Plaintiff, **ABC MORTGAGE CORPORATION**, (Hereafter "**ABC**"), pursuant to 1.10, 1.130, 1.210(a) and 1.140(b)(6), Fla. R. Civ. P, alleging as grounds thereof as follows: to wit and Federal Rules of Civil Procedure 12 (b):

1. On or around May 10, 2010, Plaintiff filed a complaint against
Defendant, James Henry to foreclosure on the subject property located on 500 S Andrews Avenue, Apartment 300, Fort. Lauderdale, Florida 33301.
2. (briefly state more facts, that you want the judge to know about the case).
3. (List facts as why the court should dismiss the complaint:

Examples are legal defenses which include: lack of subject matter jurisdiction, failure to join an indispensable party, lack of jurisdiction over the person, improper venue, improper

---

8 Federal Rules of Civil Procedure.

service of process, failure to state a claim upon which relief can be granted, laches, unjust enrichment, Violation of Fair Debt Collection Practice Act, Plaintiff has no standing to sue and/or unjust enrichment, etc).

Wherefore Defendant requests that this court will enter an order dismissing Plaintiff's complaint with prejudice and assess all costs and fee against Plaintiff. I **HEREBY CERTIFY** that a copy of this motion to dismiss was served on Plaintiff's attorney at _____ *(address of Plaintiff attorney and name of Plaintiff's attorney)* by U.S. Mail on _____*(date and month and year, it was mailed)*.

_____

Date

_____
Your name

_____
Address

_____
Telephone

Sample Answer and Affirmative Defenses

IN THE CIRCUIT COURT OF THE XXXXX JUDICIAL CIRCUIT OF THE STATE OF FLORIDA, IN AND FOR XXXXX COUNTY CIVIL DIVISION *(put your court information here)*

ABC MORTGAGE CORPORATION

VS.   CASE NUMBER 10-653XXX

JAMES HENRY, ET AL

_____/

DEFENDANT'S JAMES HENRY ANSWER AND AFFIRMATIVE DEFENSES AGAINST PLAINTIFF'S COMPLAINT

NOW INTO COURT, comes the Defendant James Henry (Hereinafter "**HENRY**" or "**DEFENDANT**"), and file this answer and affirmative defenses against Plaintiff's Complaint filed by **ABC MORTGAGE CORPORATION**, (Hereafter "**ABC**"), pursuant to 1.10, 1.130, 1.210(a) and 1.140(b)(6), Fla. R. Civ. P, alleging as grounds thereof as follows: to wit and Federal Rules of Civil Procedure 12 (b):

Answer

As to paragraph 1, 2, 3, 4 and 5, Defendant denies the allegations and requires strike proof thereof.

As to paragraph 7, Defendant is without knowledge and requires strike proof thereof.

As to the remaining paragraph, Defendant admits those allegations.

Affirmative defenses

Defendant James Henry asserts the following defenses:
1. Lost Note- Plaintiff is barred because Plaintiff does not have the note to foreclosure on the subject property.

In Plaintiff's complaint, Plaintiff count 2 admit that Plaintiff lost the note or cannot establish its whereabouts. (*use your facts here to establish lost note*).

2. Lack of Standing- Plaintiff is barred from recovery because Plaintiff does not have standing to sue.

3. Failure to join an indispensible party- Plaintiff is barred from recovery because Plaintiff has failed to join an indispensible party to the lawsuit. The mortgage attached reflects that Mortgage Electronic Registration System (MERS) is the nominee lender. However, ABC corporation is bringing the action. Because Plaintiff fails to attach an indispensible party, Plaintiff is barred from recovery. (*you may want to add your facts here*).

4. Violation of Truth in Lending 16 U.S.C. § 1601 (TILA).
Plaintiff is barred from recovery because the mortgage is in violation of 16 U.S.C. § 1601. When Defendant, Henry obtained the mortgage from Plaintiff, Plaintiff did not comply with TILA. The TILA violation includes: (*Add relevant Facts*).

5. RESPA VIOLATION. Plaintiff is barred from recover because Plaintiff has violated, Real Estate Settlement Procedural Act, RESPA,12 U.S.C. § 2601. (*add more facts to it, like your facts and check your statute and federal statutes to incorporate into this form*).

6. HOEPA VIOLATION. Plaintiff is barred from recovery because Plaintiff has violated Homeownership Equity Protection Act, HOEPA (16 U.S.C. § 1639)

7. UNCONSCIONABILITY. Plaintiff is barred from recovery because the loan terms are Unconscionable. (*add facts to show how the loan terms of the loan were crazy and unfair to you. For example, Plaintiff offered you a rate of 14%, even though you had a credit score of over 700. Additionally, Plaintiff funded your loan, within two days and without any documentation*).

8. UNFAIR AND DECEPTIVE FAIR TRADE PRACTICE Plaintiff is barred from recovery because Plaintiff exercise is Unfair and Deceptive Fair Trade Practice. (*Add facts to show how Plaintiff advertised or made false promise to you and it* *enticed you in obtaining the loan. And it turn out the adver-tisement was false and misleading).*

9. *(Add more affirmative defenses, by reading through Chapter 12 of this book).*

Wherefore Defendant requests that this court will enter an order dismissing and/or barring Plaintiff against judgment against Defendant.

Respectfully Submitted,

_____

Your Name

I **hereby certify** that a copy of this answer and affirma-tive was served on Plaintiff's attorney at _____ *(address of Plaintiff attorney and name of Plaintiff's attor-ney)* by U.S. Mail on _____*(date and month and year, it was mailed).*

_____

Date

_____

Your name

_____

Address

_____

Telephone

Sample Motion for Enlargement of Time

IN THE CIRCUIT COURT OF THE SEVENTEENTH JUDICIAL CIRCUIT OF THE STATE OF FLORIDA, IN AND FOR BROWARD COUNTY CIVIL DIVISION

ABC MORTGAGE CORPORATION

VS.   CASE NUMBER 10-65XXXXX

JAMES HENRY, ET AL

_____/

DEFENDANT'S JAMES HENRY MOTION FOR ENGLAREMENT OF TIME

COMES NOW, Defendant, James Henry and files this Motion for enlargement of time to respond to (*Plaintiff's complaint, Plaintiff's request to produce, Plaintiff's request for admission*) and offers the following support for the motion:

1. On or about __2010, Defendant was served with Plaintiff's complaint
2. On or about _____ (*briefly described some of the facts of the case*).
3. Defendant is requesting additional time to respond to plaintiff's (*List what you are requesting the extension for*).
4. Defendant will need additional time to respond to Plaintiff's (*what you are responding to*) because Defendant needs additional time to review legal documents to mount a defense, or Defendant needs additional time because Defendant is going through some personal issues that will not allow Defendant to focus on this stage of litigation.
5. Defendant is not filing this motion for enlargement of time to delay or abuse the judicial system.
6. Granting Defendant's motion for enlargement of time, will not prejudice the plaintiff.

7. The court should grant the motion for enlargement of time of _____ (*list what the extension is for, request to produce, response to Plaintiff's complaint, and list why the court should grant the motion for enlargement of time*).

Wherefore Defendant requests that this court will enter an order granting Defendant's motion.

Respectfully Submitted,

_____

Your Name

I **hereby certify** that a copy of this motion for enlargement of time was served on Plaintiff's attorney at _____ (*address of Plaintiff attorney and name of Plaintiff's attorney*) by U.S. Mail on _____ (*date and month and year, it was mailed*).

_____

Date

_____

Your name

_____

Address

_____

Telephone

Sample Request to Produce

IN THE CIRCUIT COURT OF THE SEVENTEENTH JUDICIAL CIRCUIT OF THE STATE OF FLORIDA, IN AND FOR BROWARD COUNTY CIVIL DIVISION

ABC MORTGAGE CORPORATION

VS.   CASE NUMBER 10-65XXXX

JAMES HENRY, ET AL

_____/

DEFENDANT'S JAMES HENRY REQUEST FOR PRODUCTION OF DOCUMENTS

COMES NOW, the Defendant JAMES HENRY, a prose litigant and pursuant to Rule 1.350, Florida Rules of Civil Procedure (*add your State Rule*), and requests Plaintiff to produce the following documents to be inspected at Defendant's address located at _____(*put the property address that is subject to foreclosure*).

DEFINITIONS

1. The words "you", "yours" and/or "yourselves" means. (*State the name of your lender*), and any other entity similarly situated or other persons acting, or purporting to act, on behalf of (*state the name of your lender*).
2. The singular shall include the plural and vice versa; the terms "and" and "or" shall be both conjunctive and disjunctive; and the term "including" means "including without limitation."
3. "Date" shall mean the exact date, month and year, if ascertainable, if not, the best approximation of the date (based upon relationship with other events).
4. The word "documents" shall mean any writing, recording, or photograph in your actual or constructive

possession, custody, care and control, which pertain directly or indirectly, in whole or in part, either to any of the subjects listed below or to any other matter relevant to the issues in this action, or which are themselves listed below as specific documents, including, but not limited to: correspondence, memoranda, notes, messages, diaries, minutes, books, reports, charts, ledgers, invoices, computer printouts, computer memory, e-mails, microfilms, videotapes or tape recordings.

5. "Agent" shall mean any agent, employee, officer, director, attorney, independent contractor or any other person acting at the direction of or on behalf of another.

6. "Person" shall mean any individual, corporation, proprietorship, partnership, trust, association or any other entity.

7. The words "pertain to" or "pertaining to" mean: relates to, refers to, contains, concerns, describes, embodies, mentions, constitutes, constituting, supports, corroborates, demonstrated, proves, evidences, shows, refutes, disputes, rebuts, controverts or contradicts.

8. The term "third party" or "third parties" refers to individuals or entities that are not parties to this action.

9. The term "action" shall mean the case entitled (list the name of the case, the style of the case, the case number and the address where the court, where you are being sued, is located).

10. The term "subject property" shall mean (*state the address of the property being foreclosure upon*).

11. For purpose of this document, the word "identify", means the name and address of the custodian of the document, the location of the document, and the general description of the document, including (a) the type, general subject matter, author and addresses of document (correspondence, memorandum, facsimile etc.), (b) the general subject matter of the document.

12. For purpose of this production, the word "describe," means an act, event, occurrence, or course of conduct, rule or procedure.

    A. Please write in detail all facts relating to such act, event, or occurrences, course of conduct, rule or procedure;

    B. Please provide a detail description of time and place of each such act, event, occurrence or course of conduct;

    C. Please completely identify all documents relating to or referring thereto;

    D. Please completely identify all persons present or having knowledge thereto.

13. For purpose of this production, "THE MORTGAGE" attributes to the mortgage dated (*list the day, month and year, your mortgage was dated*), by (*borrower's name here*), which mortgage was executed and delivered to (*name of mortgage here*), and is for the principal amount of $(*list your principle amount*), and which was recorded on (*list the date your mortgage was recorded*), in Official Records Book (*list the book and page it was recorded*) of the Public Records of (*list your county, town and state*).

14. "THE NOTE" means (*look to see what type of note you obtained. Ie. Adjustable note, interest only etc and write it in here*) dated (*list the day, month and year of the note*), by (*borrower's name*), and executed and delivered to (*name of lender*) for the principal amount of $(*amount borrower obtained*).

Documents and Items Requested

REQUEST NO. 1: Please provide me, Defendant, with all documents in your (Plaintiff's) possession or which Plaintiff has available regarding the note and mortgage that is subject to this lawsuit. This includes:

    A.   Copies of all contracts, documentation regarding truth in lending and other disclosure forms that are required by the Federal Statute and State Statute (if applicable) the date Defendant closed on the subject loan. Additionally, please provide me with copies of all contracts with all attorneys that you have retained for defending this action or for obtaining TARP (funding from the Federal Government, if your institution received the TARP funding).

B. Please provide copies of all receipt for payments that Defendant made against this mortgage that is now subject to this action.

C. Please provide copies of written documentation that you, Plaintiff, received or sent to Defendant.

D. Provide me with a written itemized transaction history. This includes all debts, credit or payments on the note and mortgage that are subject to this action.

REQUEST NO. 2: Provide all written communications, and notices relating to the Defendant's account, from third parties such as Fannie Mae/Freddie Mac or any investor that has an interest with this mortgage and note.

REQUEST NO. 3: Provide all copies of training materials which shows evidence of your (Plaintiff's) service obligations to your investors or Fannie Mae/Freddie Mac, which is subject to this mortgage and note.

REQUEST NO. 4: Provide copies of all internal memorandum, training materials or other documentation which Plaintiff has distributed or received from Fannie Mae/Freddie Mac or an investor relating to Plaintiff's servicing obligation for this mortgage and note.

REQUEST NO. 5: Provide copies of all written communication relating to all actives from Plaintiff and regarding Defendant's mortgage and note, with respect to this lawsuit.

REQUEST NO. 6: Provide a copy of the mortgage Loan Purchase Agreement.

REQUEST NO. 7: If this is a trust agreement, then please provide the pooling and servicing agreement that is now subject to this lawsuit. If this agreement is a securitized or CDO, please provide those agreement as also.

REQUEST NO. 8: Please provide a copy of all agreements that were sent to the Securities and Exchange Commission. This includes public disclosure requirement or an application.

CERTIFICATE OF SERVICE

I HEREBY CERTIFY that a true and correct copy of the foregoing has been furnished on,*(put the date and month and year you mailed it to the Lender's attorney here)* by U.S. Mail to: *(put the Lender's attorney name and address here)*.

_____

(put your name and address here)

Sample Request for Admission

IN THE CIRCUIT COURT OF THE SEVENTEENTH JUDICIAL CIRCUIT OF THE STATE OF FLORIDA, IN AND FOR BROWARD COUNTY CIVIL DIVISION

ABC MORTGAGE CORPORATION

VS.   CASE NUMBER 10-65XXXXX

JAMES HENRY, ET AL

_____/

DEFENDANT'S JAMES HENRY REQUEST FOR ADMISSION

Defendant James Henry, requests that Plaintiff ABC Mortgage Corporation, admit or deny the following statements of law. If Plaintiff objects to the questions, then Plaintiff must state the reason for the objection. Plaintiff must either deny, or set the details for the reason the Plaintiff cannot truthfully admit or deny the matter.

1. Admit that you have no standing to sue.
2. Admit that you are not in possession of the note.
3. Admit that you violated (*name your state*) Statute and Federal Statute when you serviced or approved the loan.
4. Admit that you are in violation of TILA.
5. Admit that you are in violation of RESPA (*add other defenses here, like Statute of* Fraud *(if applicable)* **HELPFUL HINT-** *Use other defenses from your affirmative defenses and look at other affirmative defenses covered in this book, Chapter 12.*
6. Admit that you have no supporting or authenticate documents or evidence to sustain your summary judgment.
7. Admit that prior to bringing this lawsuit, you have not complied with certain condition precedent.

8. Admit that you failed to provide Defendant, (*put your name here*) with proper notice.
9. Admit that you are charging illegal fees to the mortgage.
10. Admit that you did not obtain an assignment of mortgage from (*previous lender's name*) prior to the filing of the foreclosure. (*Only add this sentence in, if the lender has or claimed to have been assigned the loan*).
11. Admit that you have not complied with (quote whichever statutes you are relying upon. It could be both federal and state statutes).

Respectfully Submitted,

_____

Your Name

I hereby certify that a copy of this request for admission was served on Plaintiff's attorney at _____(*address of Plaintiff attorney and name of Plaintiff's attorney*) by U.S. Mail on _____(*date and month and year, it was mailed*).

_____

Date

_____
Your name

_____
Address

_____
Telephone

Sample Motion for Mediation

IN THE CIRCUIT COURT OF THE SEVENTEENTH JUDICIAL CIRCUIT OF THE STATE OF FLORIDA, IN AND FOR BROWARD COUNTY CIVIL DIVISION

ABC MORTGAGE CORPORATION

VS.   CASE NUMBER 10-XXXX6

JAMES HENRY, ET AL

_____/

Motion for Mediation

Comes now Defendant, James Henry, and files with this court a Motion for mediation as grounds to follow:

1. This is an action for an action for foreclosure
2. Defendant was served on (*put the date you were served*) with Plaintiff's complaint.
3. (*List more facts that will be relevant to the mediation*).
4. The property that is being foreclosed upon is Defendant's personal home.
5. Mediation would help the parties to resolve the foreclosure issue.
6. (*List more reasons that the court should grant the mediation*).

WHEREFORE, Defendant requests that the court order both Plaintiff and defendant to attend mediation within 60 days from the date the order has been granted.

Respectfully submitted,

_____

Your Name

I hereby certify that a copy of this motion for enlargement of time was served on Plaintiff's attorney at _____ (*address of Plaintiff attorney and name of Plaintiff's attorney*) by U.S. Mail on _____(*date and month and year, it was mailed*).

_____

Date

_____
Your name

_____
Address

_____
Telephone

Sample Motion to Compel Discovery

IN THE CIRCUIT COURT OF THE SEVENTEENTH JUDICIAL CIRCUIT OF THE STATE OF FLORIDA, IN AND FOR BROWARD COUNTY CIVIL DIVISION

ABC MORTGAGE CORPORATION

VS.   CASE NUMBER 10-00XXXXX

JAMES HENRY, ET AL

_____/

Motion to Compel _____ (*Insert which discovery you need to compel Plaintiff to respond to. If it is an admission, then call it motion to compel admission, if it is interrogatories, then call it motion to compel interrogatories, if it is request to produce, then call it motion to compel request for production*)

NOW COMES, Defendant, James Henry, a pro se litigant, hereby files this Motion to Compel (insert which discovery it is) and hereby states as follows:

1. On _____ (*date, Defendant was served with Plaintiff's foreclosure lawsuit*).
2. On _____ Defendant filed a motion to dismiss the lawsuit.
3. On _____, the court denied and Defendant immediately filed a response, by filing an answer and affirmative defenses.
4. On _____, Defendant served his first request for _____-(list the discovery that was served).
5. According to Florida Statute, Section _____ (*List the statute that you rely upon in your state that gives you the authority to serve Plaintiff with discovery document. If you are in the state of Florida, See Florida Rules of Civil Procedure 1.28-1.380*).

6. The Defendant has not received any response to the discovery.

7. Additionally, Plaintiff has not objected to the discovery of (*put which one, admission, production, interrogatories*).

Defendant respectfully request that this Court enter an order compelling Plaintiff to respond to the _____ (*list which discovery*) within 10 days from the order granting.

SAMPLE MOTION TO STRIKE

IN THE CIRCUIT COURT OF THE SEVENTEENTH JUDICIAL CIRCUIT OF THE STATE OF FLORIDA, IN AND FOR BROWARD COUNTY CIVIL DIVISION

ABC MORTGAGE CORPORATION

VS.   CASE NUMBER 10-653121

JAMES HENRY, ET AL

_____/

Motion to Strike

COMES NOW, the Defendant, pro se undersigned and hereby files this Motion to Strike, Plaintiff's (*Add what you are striking i.e. summary judgment, summary judgment hearing, request for production, plaintiff's affidavit*) and in support of this Motion to Strike states the following:

(1)   This action is based upon a foreclosure.
(2)   The Property that Plaintiff is attempting to foreclosure is located at (*put the address of the pending foreclosure property here*).
(3)   The property is Defendant's primary resident.
(4)   On (*list some facts that relating to the case that will be helpful to you and you want the judge to consider*).

WHEREFORE, Defendant requests that the court grant Defendant's Motion to Strike Plaintiff's (*name which pleading you are trying to strike*).

Respectfully Submitted,

_____

Your Name

I hereby certify that a copy of this motion to Strike Plaintiff _____was served on Plaintiff's attorney at _____*(address of Plaintiff attorney and name of Plaintiff's attorney)* by U.S. Mail on _____*(date and month and year, it was mailed)*.

_____

Date

_____
Your name

_____
Address

_____
Telephone

Sample of Interrogatories to Serve Upon Plaintiff Below is a sample of Defendant's Notice of Serving Interrogatories to Plaintiff. This is a discovery request that also should have specific definitions and instructions like the Request to Produce Documents. Interrogatories are questions that you ask the Plaintiff and the Plaintiff has to answer them in writing and under oath.

IN THE CIRCUIT COURT OF THE SEVENTEENTH JUDICIAL CIRCUIT OF THE STATE OF FLORIDA, IN AND FOR BROWARD COUNTY CIVIL DIVISION

ABC MORTGAGE CORPORATION

VS.   CASE NUMBER 10-65XXXX

JAMES HENRY, ET AL

_____/

NOTICE OF SERVING INTERROGATORIES

DEFENDANT, JAMES HENRY, as a prose litigant, propounds the following Interrogatories to the PLAINTIFF, ABC MORTGAGE CORPORATION, to be answered within thirty (30) days from receipt hereof, pursuant to Rule 1.340 of the Florida Rules of Civil Procedure.

CERTIFICATE OF SERVICE

I HEREBY CERTIFY that a true and correct copy of the foregoing have been furnished by U.S. Mail or fax this __ day of _____, 2010, to all parties listed on the attached service list.

_____

(sign your name, put your name
and put your address here)

SERVICE LIST

*(Put the name of the
Lender's Attorney here, along with the
Lender's attorney's address).*

*(If there are additional
parties, then add their
name to the service list).*

INTERROGATORIES

1. Please write the name and address of every person that will be answering or will be providing answers to these interrogatories
2. Since you have claimed to be the owner of the note or mortgage, please provide a detailed explanation as to why you possess any interest in the subject property that is now in foreclosure. By doing so, please provide documentation to support your allegations or a detailed explanation to support your allegation.
3. Please identify whether you are the servicer of the loan, mortgage or note. And if you are the servicer of the loan, then provide full documentation to me proving that the investor of the loan gave you full authority to initiate foreclosure.
4. If an assignment of mortgage took place, then provide me with the contract that you used to obtain the assignment. Please provide me with the name, address and phone number of the assignor.
5. If there were multiple assignments of mortgage, then provide me with all the names, and addresses and contracts of each and every assignment, from the date the home was purchased by me to today's date.
6. Please provide the name of the investor that owns the note. Please include a copy of the documentation reflecting that the investor is the true owner. Please provide the full contact number, name and address of the investor(s) who own the note.

7. Please provide in full detail, what type of loan this is (i.e. Fannie Mae, Freddie Mac, Ginne Mae, private investor, Jumbo Loan). If the loan is Fannie Mae, then provide a full contact and name for the contact person. If the loan is Freddie Mac, then provide a full contact. Whichever entity backs this loan, please provide the contact name and address.

8. Please provide a full detail on whether this loan has been pooled or sold in a trust, a CDO, a securitized loan (*list the other mortgage product that might have been sold. E.g. Pooling and trust agreement*) and if so, then list the date and address and year, and full description on what date the loan has been pooled, sold or packages in the secondary market.

9. Please provide a full detail on whether you obtained any TARP Funding from the Obama Administration. List the date you obtained it and list the requirement of obtaining it and list the commitment you made to obtain the fund (i.e. that you would help troubled borrowers save their home from foreclosure). List also the corporate office or agency name and full contact including phone number and address of the representative who secured the TARP funding.

10. Please state whether the note and/or mortgage was ever insured by a private insurance company or a government entity. Also provide the name and full address and explain in detail the benefit and requirements of obtaining the fund and when the proceeds would be paid to you and who the beneficial is on the insurance.

11. Please explain and describe, for the subject mortgage loan, the relationships among parties (including you, the original lender, all prior owners, and all holders or possessor, any depository, and all servicer, any custodian, and any Special Purpose Vehicle or Special Purpose Entity, etc.)

12. Please identify each and every document which contains an obligation or option to repurchase the subject mortgage loan and explain fully the terms, conditions, costs to be incurred or paid by each party upon

repurchase and whether and by whom, and from whom, the mortgage loan were ever repurchased.

13. Please state, for the note and mortgage, whether and as of what date you secured the originals thereof and from whom providing the contact name, full legal name, address, and phone number of each such party.

14. Please identify each and every document you obtained or reviewed in connection with your taking assignment of the note and/or mortgage and specify for each such document whether you maintain the original or a copy thereof.

15. Please state all parties who have provided servicing of the mortgage loan and provide the contact name, full legal name, address, and phone number of each such party and the dates each began servicing the loan.

16. Please state for the history of the mortgage loan, the persons or entity who at any time collected mortgage payments specifying the applicable dates each such person or entity did so collect and specifying the full legal name, address, and phone number of each such party.

17. Please state for the history of the mortgage loan, on whose behalf mortgage payments were collected specifying the applicable dates collection was made for each such person or entity and specifying the full legal name, address, and phone number of each such party.

18. Please state for the history of the mortgage loan, a full description of the disposition of collected mortgage payments specifying any person or entity to which mortgage payments were delivered, transferred, or paid, the applicable dates each such person or entity received the payments and further specify the full legal name, address, and phone number of each such party.

19. Please identify a representative of Plaintiff with knowledge of the facts necessary to respond to each of the interrogatories contained herein or if more than one, identify each such representative providing the name, address and telephone number for each with a brief summary of each representative's knowledge in this matter.

VERIFICATIONS OF ANSWERS TO INTERROGATORIES

STATE OF _____

COUNTY OF _____

BEFORE ME, the undersigned authority, personally appeared Plaintiff, *NAME*, and states that the answers to the interrogatories are true and correct to the best of their knowledge, information, and belief and subscribed their name hereto in certification thereof.

_____

NAME

Sworn to and subscribed before me this ____ day of _____, 2010, by _____, who is personally known to me, or produced a (*put the state the id was issued*) driver's license as identification.

_____

Notary Public
State of _____ at Large
My Commission Expires:

SAMPLE OF DEFENDANT'S MOTION TO CANCEL PLAINTIFF'S FORECLOSURE SALE (use this if there is a sale date pending. It can get you around 120 days day or even more. At times the judge will allow the sale to be rescheduled or the sale may get cancelled completely. If the sale is cancelled completely, then plaintiff would have to file a motion to reset it, which means more time for you).

IN THE CIRCUIT COURT OF THE SEVENTEENTH JUDICIAL CIRCUIT OF THE STATE OF FLORIDA, IN AND FOR BROWARD COUNTY CIVIL DIVISION

ABC MORTGAGE CORPORATION

VS.   CASE NUMBER 10-65XXXX

JAMES HENRY, ET AL

_____/

DEFENDANT'S JAMES HENRY, MOTION TO CANCEL PLAINTIFF'S FORECLOSURE SALE DATE

Defendant, James Henry, a pro se litigant, files this Motion to Cancel Plaintiff's Foreclosure Sale, and in support hereof, states as follows:

1. This is an action by (*name your lender*) to foreclose on a mortgage on certain real property located in (*name where your property is located*).
2. The Property is the Defendant homestead property.
3. A Final Summary Judgment in Foreclosure was entered in this case on (*name the year the and month the judgment was entered*) pursuant to which a foreclosure sale date of thereafter and was ordered by the Court.
4. After Summary Judgment, Plaintiff and Defendant came into an agreement that Defendant would apply and obtain a loan modification. (*Add your facts that you want the judge to consider in cancelling the sale on your home*).

5. Defendant submitted the loan modification to Plaintiff around May 2010 (*put the month and year if applicable, or change the facts to reflect your situation*).

6. Plaintiff advised the defendant that the paperwork for the modification was received and Plaintiff would approve the modification.

7. Since Plaintiff and Defendant will work on a resolution for Defendant to save the home, then it would be unfair for the property to be sold. (*insert your facts here*)

8. There is a pending sale for October 28, 2010 and the defendant need additional time to accept and perform under the pending or preapproved Loan Modification. (*Add your facts here and give you sale date here*).

9. However, the defendant needs time to accept and make his first payment.

10. The relief requested herein is made in good faith and not for the purpose delaying justice or any other improper purpose, and such relief is requested on an emergency basis only because the Property will otherwise be sold at a foreclosure auction within _____ (*put how many days before property is sold*) from the date hereof.

WHEREFORE, the Defendant, James Henry respectfully request that the Court enter an order cancelling the foreclosure sale scheduled for October 28, 2010 to allow Plaintiff the additional time for loss mitigation review, and for such other and further relief as the Court may deem just and proper.

I HEREBY CERTIFY that a true and correct copy of the foregoing have been furnished by U.S. Mail or fax this ____ day of _____, 20____, to all parties listed on the attached service list.

_____

(*put your name and address here*)

SERVICE LIST

Case No.: (*put the case name here***)**

*(Put the Lender's attorney's
name and address here).*

*(If other parties are on the
pleading, add their names here too)*.

SAMPLE OF SUGGESTION OF BANKRUPTCY (use this if you filed for chapter 13 or chapter 7. This will put the court on notice of your automatic stay).

IN THE CIRCUIT COURT OF THE SEVENTEENTH JUDICIAL CIRCUIT OF THE STATE OF FLORIDA, IN AND FOR BROWARD COUNTY CIVIL DIVISION

ABC MORTGAGE CORPORATION

VS.   CASE NUMBER 10-XXXX121

JAMES HENRY, ET AL

_____/

SUGGESTION OF BANKRUPTCY

Defendant JAMES HENRY, has filed a petition for relief under Title 11, United States Code, in the United States Bankruptcy Court for the (*put the district your filed in here*) District of (*put the state the district is*) that has been assigned case number (*place your bankruptcy case number here*) and relief was ordered on (*put the date the relief was ordered*), and suggests that this action has been stayed by the operation of Title 11 U.S.C. § 362.

CERTIFICATE OF SERVICE

I HEREBY CERTIFY that a true and correct copy of the foregoing have been furnished by U.S. Mail or fax this ____ day of _____, 20____, to all parties listed on the attached service list.

_____

(*put your name and address here*)

SERVICE LIST

Case No.: *(put the case name here***)**

*(Put the Lender's attorney's
name and address here).*

*(If other parties are on the
pleading, add their names here too).*

IN THE CIRCUIT COURT OF THE SEVENTEENTH JUDICIAL CIRCUIT OF THE STATE OF FLORIDA, IN AND FOR BROWARD COUNTY CIVIL DIVISION

ABC MORTGAGE CORPORATION

VS.   CASE NUMBER 10-XXXX121

JAMES HENRY, ET AL

_____/

NOTICE OF HEARING

(Motion Calendar)

PLEASE TAKE NOTICE that the Defendant, James Henry, in the above-styled cause by and through the undersigned attorney, will call up for hearing the following:

JAMES HENRY'S MOTION TO DISMISS THE COMPLAINT

Before the Honorable Judge (*put the name of the judge here*) on (*put the date, time and the room number where the judge holds the hearing*) of the (*put the district the court is located here*) Courthouse, located at (*put the address of the courthouse here*).

PLEASE GOVERN YOURSELF ACCORDINGLY

_____

(put your name and address here)
(make sure you sign your name above)

CERTIFICATE OF SERVICE

I HEREBY CERTIFY that a true and correct copy of the fore-going have been furnished by U.S. Mail or fax this ____ day of _____, 20__, to all parties listed on the attached service list.

SERVICE LIST

(put the name and address of the lender's Attorney here)

In accordance with the Americans with Disabilities Act of 1990, all persons who are disabled and who need special accommodations to participate in this proceeding because of that disability should contact the ADA Coordinator at, *(put your court address here)*, not later than five (5) business days prior to the proceeding.

Teisha Powell, Law Offices P.A.
ATTORNEY AT LAW
REAL ESTATE LAW & LITIGATION & BANKRUPTCY

200 SOUTH ANDREWS AVENUE, STE 703
FT. LAUDERDALE, FL 33301
WWW.STOPFORECLOSURENOWINFLORIDA.COM
Telephone: (561) XXX-XXX   Facsimile: (954) XXX

AUTHORIZATION FOR RELEASE OF
INFORMATION AND RECORDS

November 27, 2009

Loan Servicer [Mortgage Co.] Name: **JC BANK OF FORECLOSURE**

Loan Number: 000123456789

The following person(s) is (are) the LEGAL BORROWER(s) on the property address listed below:

Name #1: Joe Doe Social Security Number #1: 123-43-1234

Name #2: Jane Doe Social Security Number #000-00-0000

Property Address: 1234 Apple Street City: Fort Lauderdale State: Florida Zip Code: 33068

I (WE), hereby authorize the above referenced Loan Servicer, successors, assigns, agents, employees and associates, and their respective servicing companies to release and discuss any and all matters pertaining to the aforementioned loan with Teisha Powell, Law Office, P.A XXXX *(address of law Firm)*, its attorneys, agents, and employees and in connection with, but not limited to, loan mitigation, workouts, resolutions, settlements and indebtedness.

_____   _____

Borrower(s) Signature   Borrower(s) Signature

_____   _____

Date   Date

Bibliography

Ellis, Stephen. (2009) *The Foreclosure Survival Guide: Keep Your House or Walk Away With Money in Your Pocket*.
Garner, Bryan A. (2007) *Federal Rules of Civil Procedure*.
http://www.realtytrac.com/foreclosure-laws/foreclosure-laws-comparison.asp
http://www.flsb.uscourts.gov/
http://www.hud.gov
http://en.wikipedia.org/wiki/Homeownership_in_the_United_States

www.ingramcontent.com/pod-product-compliance
Lightning Source LLC
Chambersburg PA
CBHW071428170526
45165CB00001B/435